The Spokesman
Money Troubles … War Crimes

Edited by Ken Coates
Assistant Editor Tony Simpson

**Published by Spokesman for the
Bertrand Russell Peace Foundation**

Spokesman 105   2009

CONTENTS

Cover: With grateful acknowledgements to Steve Bell

ISSN 1367 7748   Printed by the Russell Press Ltd., Nottingham, UK   ISBN 978 0 85124 769 4

Subscriptions
Institutions £35.00
Individuals £20.00 (UK)
£25.00 (ex UK)

Back issues available
on request

A CIP catalogue record
for this book is available
from the British Library

Published by the
Bertrand Russell Peace
Foundation Ltd.,
Russell House
Bulwell Lane
Nottingham NG6 0BT
England
Tel. 0115 9784504
email:
elfeuro@compuserve.com
www.spokesmanbooks.com
www.russfound.org

Bertrand Russell
at Routledge

Philosopher, educational and sexual reformer, peace campaigner and prolific letter writer, author and columnist, **Bertrand Russell** was one of the most influential and widely known intellectual figures of the twentieth century. The home of more of his works than any other English language publisher, Routledge will be making its complete Bertrand Russell backlist available in the **Routledge Classics** series in 2009.

All titles NEW in September 2009

£9.99

978-0-415-48733-7

£15.99

978-0-415-47373-6

£9.99

978-0-415-48734-4

£12.99

978-0-415-48735-1

£14.99

978-0-415-48732-0

£14.99

978-0-415-48739-9

£12.99

978-0-415-48737-5

£14.99

978-0-415-48740-5

£14.99

978-0-415-48741-2

£12.99

978-0-415-47461-0

£14.99

978-0-415-48736-8

£12.99

978-0-415-48738-2

Routledge Classics: Get Inside A Great Mind

Editorial
Money Troubles …

During an intensive month of campaigning, the *Daily Telegraph* remorselessly exposed misdemeanours of Members of the House of Commons in their extensive expenses scandal. Has the focus shifted?

On Tuesday 16th June 2009 the BBC Radio Four's *Today* programme reported:

'Two Labour peers are under investigation for allegedly abusing the current allowances system, the *Today* programme has learned. Reporter Andrew Hosken examines whether the rules need to be overhauled and how the House of Lords managed, in the main, to keep out of the spotlight during the expenses row.

Andrew Hosken: Gordon Brown's recent statement on constitution reform reflected the concern that the reputations of both Houses of Parliament, not just the Commons, have been tarnished by the expenses scandal. Most Peers don't receive ministerial salaries and can claim overnight allowances for accommodation allowing them to be near Parliament. There are also daytime subsistence and office expenses. In recent weeks noble members of all three main political parties have faced accusations over their allowances.

We've learned that official complaints about two Peers are currently being investigated by Michael Pownall, the Clerk of the Parliaments, effectively the chief administrator here at the House of Lords. Both are accused of wrongly claiming thousands of pounds in overnight allowances. One of them, Lord Clarke of Hampstead, has asked Mr. Pownall to investigate; he has not returned our calls. The other, Baroness Uddin, the first female Muslim peer, insists she has done nothing wrong.

Baroness Uddin: Personally I'd like to say some things, but if you'll excuse me I shall not make any comment about my …

Andrew Hosken: (over the top of her speaking) In her first interview since the investigation began Baroness Uddin denied that she has wrongly claimed more than £80,000 in overnight allowances. Angus Robertson, an SNP MP, called for her to be investigated over allegations that she declared an empty flat in Kent to be her main residence allowing her to claim overnight subsistence on her London home.

Baroness Uddin: Generally I think it is absolutely right that people are not necessarily saying that they are sure about the rules or anything like that, they are saying that the rules are too loose and that they should be very, very specific so that people's integrity is not compromised or questioned and I think that we should just simply bring the rules up to date.

Andrew Hosken: You already have a home in East London, which is close to Parliament, so obviously there were questions asked about why you would claim a second property outside London, in Kent, as your main residence.

Baroness Uddin: Yes, I mean, I think I know that I will have to explain at an appropriate time my own personal circumstances about which, obviously, I can't go into. I'd like not to go into otherwise that circumstance would have been in the public arena.'

At this point I interrupt the BBC's account to ask what I think is a pertinent question. It is, how did we get into a situation like this? There are two ladies involved in this interview, as we shall see, and there might be other people. They progressed up the ladder into what has become, without doubt, Britain's biggest quango, the House of Lords, because New Labour saw them as an ornament, as people of achievement. Did those with genuine achievements outnumber the hangers-on? Probably not. In my mind's eye I can see them as earnest young students, or eager young socialists: bright eyed with idealism and hope for truth. Now the BBC lets us hear them, ambition realised. Clanking with mechanical avarice, they sound changed.

To return to the BBC account:

'**Andrew Hosken:** The SNP has also asked Scotland Yard to investigate a number of other Peers. This includes another Labour Peer, Baroness Thornton, a government minister in the Whips' office. For at least the past eight years Baroness Thornton has declared her main home to be in Yorkshire and for the last three years a bungalow in Shipley purchased by her mother. Since 2002, Baroness Thornton has claimed overnight allowances totalling more than £130,000 by declaring the home she shares with her husband in North London is a second property needed to help her attend the Lords.

I visited the Shipley bungalow near Leeds and spoke to Baroness Thornton's mother. She told me her daughter stays each weekend, arriving around Friday lunchtime and leaving on Sunday afternoon.

We have made several attempts to talk to Baroness Thornton.

"Hello, is Baroness Thornton in?"

She declined to talk to us and sent us a statement saying she has resented reports that she is using the address in Shipley to feather her nest. She added, "My husband and I have always intended to make our home here in Yorkshire, as our children grew up and we could do so." Although she insists she shares the ownership of the house in Shipley there is no record of this on the current Land Registry.

We spoke to Christopher Dickson, Executive Counsel to the Accountants' Disciplinary Scheme and formerly the number two at the Serious Fraud Office.

Christopher Dickson: Any potential offence would be under the Fraud Act. That requires three things to be proved. First it requires you to prove that a false statement has been made, an untrue statement. Secondly that the person who has made the statement has gained. And, thirdly that it's been done dishonestly.

Andrew Hosken: In terms of this particular case that we have shown you, Baroness Thornton, do you think that there are questions that some would need to answer?

Christopher Dickson: Yes. It does seem to me that if you apply those three tests there is something for the police to investigate. First of all, it's questionable that it is a true statement, that someone who has what appears to be their principal home in London, can properly claim overnight allowance for living in London. Secondly, the person who has done that has undoubtedly gained in the sense that they've received the overnight allowance on, no doubt, many occasions. And finally, certainly there's an issue to decide as to whether it has been dishonestly done or not. Difficult to see how that could be done honestly if one knew that one's principal residence was in fact in London.

Andrew Hosken: Most of the 738 Peers do not receive salaries and can claim allowances and office expenses. Over the years, according to several Peers, the impression has been given by the Finance Department for the Upper House that allowances should be considered as a type of salary in lieu. Baronesses Thornton and Uddin are far from being the only Peers to face questions about allowances. Baroness D'Souza is the Convenor of the crossbenchers, with more than 200 members, the second largest grouping in the Lords after Labour.

Baroness D'Souza: There is a pervasive understanding that because no salary is paid the allowances can be claimed in full. I think there is a problem there because some people interpret it one way and some people interpret it another way. What I think has happened, and this is across the House, is that there are some very few cases where people have claimed a London allowance for staying overnight and claiming that their main house is outside London when that is patently not true and perhaps they only own one house and that is a London house. Because if you live within the M25 you are not liable, you can't claim the allowance.

… **Andrew Hosken:** The wind of change is blowing as much along the red benches as the green. Transparency as well as the power to sanction errant Peers are the likely results. In the meantime, the findings of the enquiries into the two Labour Peers will be handed to the Lords' Privileges Committee for further consideration.'

Here on a thumbnail is the problem of House of Lords allowances. The Peers in question have clearly come to believe that their allowances may be deemed to be payable in lieu of a salary. Since there are 736 persons who are similarly 'entitled', this could add up to a not inconsiderable charge on the public purse. Happily, it is assumed that many Peers do not avail themselves of this largesse. But, if the conduct of other Members of Parliament, in the Lower House, is anything to go by, then it may be assumed that many do.

A week or two earlier, the appropriate disciplinary authorities suspended two members of the House of Lords because they had been found to be plying for hire, as advisors on how to modify inconvenient laws. How many other consultants, cleverer perhaps, have avoided this charge whilst still profiting from the sale of their services?

There would be a remarkably simple cure for all these problems, and all the

related questions to which they give rise. We should abolish the House of
Lords. Few would notice. None of the necessary functions of that body need
be neglected, since all could be discharged, with a limited effort, by other
responsible agencies within the system. There would be a certain cost in
flummery, since the occasion for dressing up might be diminished. It could, of
course, be devolved to school drama classes. But people who speak about
modernising British institutions do not normally mean that the Speaker of the
House of Commons should cease dressing up in a golden frock with a long
train, or that various able-bodied persons should process in front of him or her
without various beknobbed sticks and other insignia of bygone times. Perhaps
we could manage without the processions themselves, as well. The savings
might not be large, but reductions in the cost of regalia present other
advantages. They diminish the gap between representative institutions and the

---

Macavity's Not There

Macavity's a Mystery Cat: he's called the Hidden Paw –
For he's the master criminal who can defy the Law.
He's the bafflement of Scotland Yard, the Flying Squad's despair:
For when they reach the scene of crime – *Macavity's not there!*

According to the *Daily Mail* Tony Blair 'dodged possible fire over his housing
deals after hundreds of expenses claims were "accidentally shredded".' The
newspaper reported that Commons officials had destroyed these papers 'by
mistake'. They covered the period when he claimed for his Constituency
home, Myrobella, in Sedgefield, County Durham.

Picking up on this report, the *Sunday Times* alleged (May 18th 2009): 'The
documents ... were destroyed in the midst of a legal battle over whether they
should be published'. The *Sunday Times* insists that it is a criminal offence
to destroy documents which are the subject of disclosure claims, but, they
claim: 'Westminster officials say they were unaware that the files were the
subject of a legal challenge. They insist they were destroyed by mistake'.

The *Sunday Times* had requested (in January 2005) sight of Blair's claims
for £43,029 of public money covering his expenditure over three years. The
shredding came to light after the failure of a High Court appeal to block
disclosure of the expenses of fourteen Members of Parliament, including
Blair and Margaret Beckett, the former Foreign Secretary.

And when the Foreign Office find a Treaty's gone astray,
Or the Admiralty lose some plans and drawings by the way,
There may be a scrap of paper in the hall or on the stair –
But it's useless to investigate – *Macavity's not there!*
And when the loss has been disclosed, the Secret Service say:
'It *must* have been Macavity!' – but he's a mile away.

Macavity – The Mystery Cat by T. S. Eliot

people represented. All that dressing up is calculated to generate awe, and a misguided sense of respect. But if we respect people because they can parade in outlandish clothes, we are not ourselves enhanced in the process. A previous reformer understood this very well when he told his henchmen to get rid of the mace. 'Take away that bauble', he said. They did, and the heavens did not fall.

When we come to consider the earthquake which has carried away the good name of the House of Commons (if such there ever was), we encounter something more like a crisis than the exposure of wrong-doers in the House of Lords. But we should consider briefly what the endless scandals reported in the *Daily Telegraph* really represent.

One Member of Parliament spent a certain amount of taxpayers' money on mowing his lawn, shuttering his windows, and acquiring garden benches upon which to disport himself. It is difficult to justify the thought that any of these costs might be incurred in pursuit of Parliamentary duties. But they have aroused widespread outrage among his constituents, some of whose jobs are in jeopardy, and some of whose houses may indeed be repossessed in the current economic stringency. That garden bench has become an object of fury among people, and yet that garden bench is petty pilfering compared to the wholesale villainy which has raged through our banking system, as the banks have been part-nationalised or rescued, and the pension pots of their ex-directors have overflowed.

Our betters argue that the banks had to be rescued to prevent a widespread economic collapse, with a consequent meltdown in society. It was a truly Fabian gesture to cushion the fall of various chairmen with such generous cash provisions. This would guarantee a wretched form of continuity, by assuring those in authority over our money that their vital interests would not be jeopardised in the necessary effort to keep the system running. This was not easy. As George Soros told us:

'There are two features that I think deserve to be pointed out. One is that the financial system as we know it actually collapsed. After the bankruptcy of Lehman Brothers on September 15th, the financial system really ceased to function. It had to be put on artificial life support. At the same time, the financial shock had a tremendous effect on the real economy, and the real economy went into a free fall, and that was global.

The other feature is that the financial system collapsed of its own weight. That contradicted the prevailing view about financial markets, namely that they tend towards equilibrium, and that equilibrium is disturbed by extraneous forces, outside shocks. Those disturbances were supposed to occur in a random fashion. Markets were seen basically as self-correcting. That paradigm has proven to be false. So we are dealing not only with the collapse of a financial system, but also with the collapse of a worldview …'[1]

It was also a Fabian gesture to allow such generous allowances to our chosen representatives. This could enable them to posture as patriotic wage freezers instead of the beneficiaries of inflated pay awards. It becomes apparent that they denied themselves salary increases because their private allowances would offer full compensation for their public sacrifice. Mrs. Thatcher inserted the thin end of this wedge, which was, as befits him, opened greatly wider by Tony Blair:

'TONY BLAIR and accountants PricewaterhouseCoopers jointly helped push through a rule change in 2004 that brought the MPs' expenses scandal to the heart of government. Without Blair's new rule, explicitly designed to boost ministers' expenses, many of the current frontbench embarrassments would not now be an issue.

The Senior Salaries Review Board (SSRB) looked at MPs' pay, using a survey of MPs prepared by PwC, and the firm was happy to support a point that *Private Eye* understands was pushed by the then prime minister. Its report said: 'There were comments made about the rules which require ministers and other paid office holders to elect their London residence as the main residence and the constituency as their second property. The rules mean that the ACA [Additional Costs Allowance] is used against costs on a property which in many cases has been owned by the MP and his or her family for a significant number of years and where the mortgage is typically low.'

The report makes it clear that ministers had complained that because they were deemed to live in London, they could not 'flip' homes in order to claim higher expenses; they could only claim on their generally cheaper properties outside the capital. According to the review board, the rule was dropped in February 2004.

Hazel Blears' property ladder, Maria Eagle's flipping, Caroline Flint's new London flat, the bulk of Shahid Malik and Shaun Woodward's expenses and Kitty Ussher's war on 'bad taste' swirly Artex paint finishes all depend on the 2004 rule change, as do the bulk of Gordon Brown's own additional costs claims...

The former PM's support for the change was no random act of greed (indeed, Blair did not personally use the change to raise money himself, relying instead on a complex mortgage transaction on his constituency home.) He was actually trying to increase his ministers' income while publicly appearing to keep a lid on their headline pay...'[2]

But now that the truth has begun to escape, popular support for our Members of Parliament has diminished to a remarkable, if not astonishing degree. What is truly astonishing is that they have remained immune to criticism for so long, various wars notwithstanding. There is, indeed, a constitutional crisis on top of the turmoil in the economy. What these baleful events have done is to present us with an interaction, in which one crisis feeds another, and vitiates attempts to meet both. All the institutions of liberal capitalism are in jeopardy at the same time. Members of Parliament, lacking public confidence, are in no position to lay down the law to errant bankers, who can more or less deny any authority to legal initiatives of which they disapprove. Deepening slump still further aggravates the withdrawal of public trust in politicians. This was the context in which Sir Christopher Kelly, Chairman of the Committee on Standards in Public Life, who is inquiring into MPs' expenses, lamented:

> 'There can be no doubt about the extent of public anger at the way in which arrangements for the reimbursement to MPs of the expenses they incur in performing their public duties have been exploited for personal gain. Those feelings are shared by many MPs as well. It is our task to design a new set of arrangements which supports Members of Parliament properly in the performance of their very important duties, both in Westminster and in their constituencies, but does so in a way which is beyond reproach so that shattered trust can begin to be restored.'

A great deal has been said about the difficulties in which the Prime Minister finds himself. It has been pointed out that he cannot sack the Ministers with whose services he wishes to dispense, and he cannot appoint those whose help he thinks he needs. Of course not. Very minor shifts in such appointments could annul his Parliamentary majority, if quite modest measures of accountability were imposed on the wrongdoers by whom he is surrounded. Will the electors accomplish what the Parliamentary leaders have not? Can the main transgressors be removed by the vote? And, if they were, what would that leave of Parliamentary discipline amongst their replacements?

Who can stand forward as the voice of rectitude in this gathering moral shambles? It is political organisations, fuelled by patronage and shot through with corruption, that have arranged in Britain a semblance of order, ever more fractious and unstable, but none the less apparently permanent. What happens when people can see the unpleasant truth? Can the centre hold? Who hopes that it might? It has been a thieves' kitchen. That the pilfering was mainly petty does not the more commend it. The conviction begins to grow that it is time to start all over again.

Ken Coates

References
1. *New York Review of Books*, 11 June 2009.
2. *Private Eye*, 29 May 2009.

War Crimes I

Macavity's not there

*Gordon Brown MP
and others*

*Gordon Brown's
announcement of the
Chilcot Inquiry into the
Iraq War, which was to sit
in private, has been
roundly criticised, not least
by the military. This set in
train a series of u-turns,
retreats and obfuscations,
some of which are
documented here.*

On 15 June 2009, Prime Minister Gordon Brown told the House of Commons of his plans for an inquiry into the British Government's role in the Iraq War. He said:

'... I am today announcing the establishment of an independent, privy-counsellor Committee of Inquiry. It will consider the period from summer 2001 before military operations began in March 2003, and our subsequent involvement in Iraq until the end of July this year ...

The Committee of Inquiry will have access to the fullest range of information, including secret information. In other words their investigation can range across all papers all documents and all material. So the inquiry can ask for any British document to come before it and any British citizen to appear. No British document and no British witness will be beyond the scope of the inquiry. And I have asked the members of the inquiry that the final report of the inquiry will be able to disclose all but the most sensitive information, that is, all information except that which is essential to our national security.

The inquiry will receive the full co-operation of the Government – with access to all Government papers and the ability to call any witnesses – with the objective to learn the lessons from the events surrounding the conflict ... Taking into account national security considerations as the Franks Inquiry did [into the Falklands War] – for example, what might damage or reduce our military capability in the future – evidence will be heard in private. In this way also evidence given by serving and former ministers, military officers and officials will, I believe, be as full and candid as possible … The inquiry will take into account evidence submitted to previous inquiries … the committee will start work as soon as possible after the end of July, and given the complexity of the issues it will address, I am advised it will take one year. As I have made clear, the primary objective of the committee will be to identify lessons learned. The committee will not set out to apportion blame or consider issues of civil or criminal liability.'

*   *   *

The Prime Minister's announcement elicited widespread criticism, not least from military men, but also from Lord Butler, who had chaired the earlier Review of Intelligence on Weapons of Mass Destruction, which reported in July 2004.

'There is only one reason that an inquiry is being heard in private and that is to protect past and present members of this government … We have worrying questions about how intelligence was ramped up to suit Tony Blair and his cronies and their reasoning for invasion. There is no reason why intelligence officials alone should have to carry the can for this.'
Air Marshal Sir John Walker, former head of Defence Intelligence

'And they do have to look at the intelligence that Blair used … which at the end turned out to be fool's gold.'
General Sir Mike Jackson, then Chief of the General Staff

' … the Falklands was essentially a failure of intelligence. Here we are looking at something much more serious: the allegation that a British government manipulated intelligence to take part in an illegal war. There is no reason why the public should not be able to hear the witnesses and judge what they say for themselves. We should not have to depend on a group of people handpicked by the current Government. A report from a secret inquiry will look like a whitewash.'
Major General Julian Thompson, who commanded the Royal Marines in the Falklands war

'There is no prospect that an inquiry conducted entirely in private can purge the national feeling of mistrust … I reluctantly conclude that the form of the inquiry proposed by the Government has been dictated more by the Government's political interest than the national interest … The question arises: should the form of an inquiry into the actions of the

Government be determined exclusively by the Government?'
>   *Lord Butler of Brockwell, former cabinet secretary*
>   *who investigated the intelligence about Iraqi weapons*

*   *   *

Three days later, on 18 June, the Prime Minister wrote to the chairman of the new inquiry, Sir John Chilcot, and asked him to consider holding some sessions in public. He urged Sir John to hold an open session to 'explain in greater depth the significant scope and breadth of the inquiry' and to meet relatives of the servicemen killed in Iraq – either in public or in private – to explain how it would operate. He also asked him to take evidence on oath.

On 19 June, Steve Richards wrote in The Independent:

'… I am told Brown did give some thought to opening up parts if the inquiry from the beginning, but in the end he followed the advice of Alastair Campbell and Blair's other most senior advisor in No.10, Jonathan Powell, in opting for an investigation behind closed doors. Both Powell and Campbell were involved in discussions that preceded the decision. In particular Campbell warned that parts of the media would become obsessed once more in the run up to an election.

Brown also worried that an open inquiry would be seen as a snub to Blair. He had a long conversation with Blair last week. I would be amazed if this subject did not come up …'

*   *   *

On 21 June, in The Observer, *Philippe Sands QC, made a crucial distinction between national security and national embarrassment.*

'When he served on the Butler inquiry, Sir John [Chilcot] had documents before him that raised serious questions about the circumstances in which Lord Goldsmith gave his legal advice. Yet these documents – or the information they contain – have never been made public. The Butler inquiry had before it, for example, correspondence between Jack Straw and Tony Blair that undermined the case for going to war, noting Colin Powell's view that "if there was an insufficient case for a second resolution, there would be an insufficient case for the US to go unilateral". Sir John will also have seen a note written by Sir David Manning that provided a detailed account of the White House meeting of 31 January 2003 between Blair and President Bush. From this note, it looks clear that Bush and Blair recognised the inadequacy of the intelligence, had failed to make any proper preparation for post-war planning and had decided to start the war in mid-March 2003 regardless of a further Security Council resolution.

Documents like this raise issues of national embarrassment, not national security.'

* * *

John Kampfner made a salient point in The Spectator *of 24 June.*

'The charge sheet is long and yet the dock is empty. One of the most extraordinary aspects of Britain's involvement in the Iraq war has been the ability of those responsible to evade any form of reckoning. For that they have many people to thank, including incurious journalists and pliant judges. But most of all, Tony Blair is in debt to his New Labour friends for their efforts to get him off the hook – in recent days, Peter Mandelson and Gordon Brown.'

War Crimes II

Macavity –
Bang to rights

Bob Marshall-Andrews MP
Sir Menzies Campbell MP
Michael Mates MP
David Davis MP
George Galloway MP
Alan Simpson MP
Adam Price MP

Final arrangements for the Iraq Inquiry Committee under Sir John Chilcot remain fluid, as was revealed during a debate in the House of Commons on 24 June 2009, which was called by the Opposition. We reprint excerpts.

Robert Marshall-Andrews MP: Many art forms thrive as a result of warfare, but none more, as a result of the Iraq war, than the art of sophistry. The ancient art of the sophist took apparently wise and irrefutable statements which, when they are carefully examined in the context in which they are made, turn out to be utterly without reason.

There was no better example of that than the words that fell from the Prime Minister's mouth when he announced the setting up of the committee. He said that the committee was to be set up in order that we should learn the mistakes and benefit from learning the mistakes that were made, and that they should not be made again – apparently wise in itself and, in the context of what the committee must consider and decide, utterly without meaning.

The central issue for the committee must be whether the House and, through it, the British people were misled and deceived into support for an illegal war. That is the central issue. There are other tangential and peripheral issues that need to be considered. I also would like to know about the aftermath. I would very much like to know about the role of Halliburton and other companies in the so-called reconstruction of Iraq. I would like to know many of the things that have perplexed the House as to what has happened since the war, but the central issue for those who were here and voted or did not vote for the war and took that awesome responsibility is whether the House at the time was deliberately misled into an illegal war.

In that essential question two things stand out above all and must be discerned. The first centres on the so-called Downing

Street memorandum in July 2002, many months before the war began. It is a clear minute, and it shows that our man – Q – who was at the time in Washington, Richard Dearlove, reported to the then Prime Minister in these terms:

> 'Bush wanted to remove Saddam through military action justified by the conjunction of terrorism and WMD. But the intelligence and facts were being fixed around the policy.'

That was the clearest possible statement, which was echoed in the House almost exactly word for word, although he did not know of the minute, by Robin Cook at the time that he made his resignation speech – that what was happening was that the facts were being fixed around policy.

That is the first thing that requires the Prime Minister of the day to go before the committee on oath and without immunity in order to be cross-examined about that, because he came to the House almost immediately afterwards and not a word of that reached the ears of those who were listening to him and were deciding on the issue of war. It is not the only internal memorandum, but it needs to be answered.

The second matter is the legal advice that was given to Cabinet, to the House and to the House of Lords. On 7 March [2003], the Attorney-General produced an opinion that has now, like drawing teeth, been made public. That opinion was hedged with doubt throughout on whether the war was legal. Any lawyer reading it would read both between and on the lines that the Attorney-General had the gravest possible reservations about the legality of war without a United Nations resolution. Seven days later a completely different opinion was given to Cabinet and subsequently was given in the House of Lords.

If the first opinion had been made public at the time, it is highly unlikely, in my view – we have one distinguished member of that Cabinet in the Chamber, and she will be able to tell us herself – that that Cabinet universally would have voted for war in those circumstances. That is the second matter that requires investigation.

Neither of these matters requires phalanxes of lawyers. Neither affects national security in their investigation. Both are absolutely central. They can be dealt with without months of preparation, on oath and in public. There is no lesson to be learned here. The lesson of whether or not to mislead the House is a lesson very quickly learned, and the answer is simple: do not mislead the House when dealing with the intelligence and the background to war. That is what we need to decide – not the lessons for tomorrow, but the facts of the past.

The mistakes that were made have already been visited, of course, by Lord Butler and his committee, but he was constrained. Those who read the Butler report can feel the frustration that comes out of those pages that he was constrained in his brief by looking only at the intelligence, and not at the use that was made of that intelligence in the dossiers and the information that was given to the House. The frustration that his committee obviously felt was manifest in what he said in the House of Lords in an extraordinary departure from normal protocol, when he also said that the inquiry must be held in public in order to deal with the issues.

In a sense, Lord Butler has no one but himself to blame because the Butler report was written in mandarin – a language in which Robin Butler is fluent and of which some of us have a passing knowledge, but it is a foreign language to the fourth estate. So, of course, the Butler report was taken as a vindication for what it most certainly was not – that is, the political reasons and the basis for war.

May I have my three ha'p'orth of where all this sits in the events of the past weeks that have affected the House? One of the problems that lies behind the expenses debate is not that it has thrown up serious matters – it undoubtedly has – which require investigation and answer. It has also been responsible for a wave of matters that are in themselves trivial – bath plugs, paperclips, and the like. What is the reason for that? One reason, undoubtedly, is to portray this House in a Lilliputian light: to trivialise its very existence. That is it. If we allow that to happen, we deserve to be portrayed as a Lilliputian assembly, unable to control our own destiny.

It is we who were misled, many of us believe, in the preparation for the Iraq war. It was this House that was misled.

Mr. Winnick *indicated dissent.*

Mr. Marshall-Andrews: My good and hon. Friend shakes his head when I say that, but let us have an inquiry to find out, and then, at least, something that has passed between he and I will be laid to rest. It is we who were misled, if we were misled, and it is to us that the inquiry must answer and it is to us to set the terms of reference of that committee. The terms of reference are not in themselves a matter of deep jurisprudence, because they are perfectly simple: the inquiry should be open; on oath and without immunity. What is more, those against whom criticism or indictment may be made must be warned of that fact and must be represented – yes – when they give evidence before the committee.

None of that is difficult to understand; it was all enshrined in the committees that were set up under Lord Salmon and The Tribunals of Inquiry (Evidence) Act 1921, which, as my hon. Friend the Member for

Cannock Chase (Dr. Wright) pointed out, was the point at which we divested ourselves of such authority. Now, we must retain it and we must regain it. That is one reason why, if the House divides, I shall be on the Opposition side, not because I wish to vote with the Tories, but because I wish to vote for – for – an inquiry in the terms that we require it ...

Sir Menzies Campbell MP: ... I shall set out some questions that I hope the inquiry will address. What was the then Prime Minister's motive in establishing a policy of standing steadfastly by the Bush Administration? Did the Cabinet agree with that policy? Did the Cabinet ever discuss that policy? Is it the case that by July 2002 at a meeting in Downing street, the minutes of which have been leaked, as it happens to *The Daily Telegraph*, Mr. Blair was committed to military action along with the United States? Is it the case that by that meeting Mr. Blair was committed to regime change?

When did the Cabinet first discuss military action? When did the Cabinet first discuss regime change? And on how many occasions thereafter did it discuss either or both implications of Government policy? Why did the Cabinet not see the Attorney-General's full opinion of 7 March 2003, before military action commenced? Who took the decision that the Cabinet should see only the one-page answer to a question no doubt placed by arrangement in the other place? Why did the Chief of the Defence Staff insist on specific legal advice on the legality of what he was being asked to do? Was the Cabinet advised that the intelligence assessment was that war against Iraq would increase the likelihood of terrorist attacks in the United Kingdom? If not, why not? Was the Cabinet informed that the 45-minute claim related only to battlefield nuclear weapons? ...

Michael Mates MP: *[who was on the Committee of Privy Councillors under Lord Butler which conducted a 'Review of Intelligence on Weapons of Mass Destruction' and reported in July 2004]* ... The right hon. and learned Member for North-East Fife (Sir Menzies Campbell) asked a number of questions. I know most of the answers, because we were shown all the evidence. We had to go into the legal aspects of the matter from an intelligence point of view, and we reported on that. However, we were constrained from reporting on them other than from that point of view. I remember that when we asked the Attorney-General a specific question, he said, 'Well, there was no intelligence aspect to that question, so I do not have to answer it.' Sir John [Chilcot] must have a broad canvas to work on.

I have seen advice from the Attorney-General that I do not believe the right hon. Member for Birmingham, Ladywood (Clare Short) has seen, because it was not shown to the Cabinet. Some of it was leaked, and all of it was given to us, but we were constrained from reporting on it. That was not for reasons of national security but because if we had tried to, someone would have said that it was none of our business. That needs to be put right so that the Chilcot inquiry can examine all the matters that I have mentioned.

Regime change loomed large in the arguments about the legality of the war, as did [UN] resolution 1441. Papers laying everything out have flown between very senior Government representatives and Ministers, which will make certain people's eyes water when they see them. Our inquiry saw all those things, and the Chilcot committee must see them and be able to report on them. Five or six years on, it is not a question of national security any more. It is about what advice was given to Ministers and what their reaction to it was – did they accept it, or did they ignore it?

One issue to consider is the resignation of a legal adviser to the Foreign Office, who was not content with the Attorney-General's advice. That is in the public domain, but the reasons behind it are not. That may explain why the FCO was largely excluded from the latter stages of the discussions and the decision taking, most notably when Tony Blair, the Prime Minister, met President Bush in Washington with his coterie of No. 10 advisers and Sir Christopher Meyer, our ambassador there, was excluded from the meeting. If it is not the job of Her Majesty's ambassador to be there to report from the American perspective, I do not know what is, but he was not permitted to go to that meeting. I shall not repeat myself, but we have seen the accounts of that meeting, whereas others who should have seen them have not. Sir John must be able to bring all that out.

Why is there no one with some legal expertise on the committee? We need that sort of expertise among its members, so it seems strange it is missing from those people who have been chosen, although, like others, I am in no way criticising them.

My last point is about the intelligence, political and machinery of government aspects that led to the way in which the decisions were taken, which we were able to report on more substantially. In fact, our comments on that were perhaps some of our most trenchant. Perhaps the hon. and learned Member for Medway did not get the bit in mandarin, because we were highly critical of the style of government that had led to no notes being taken and no record being made.

Mr. Marshall-Andrews: The passage to which I think the right hon. Gentleman is referring is exactly the mandarin passage that I had in mind, when Lord Butler said that, taking everything together, the committee was 'surprised' that none of the intelligence being placed before the Government was reflected in the statements being made. The word 'surprised' in mandarin does not mean: 'Good Lord! Is that the time?' It means: 'It is absolutely inconceivable that anything like this could happen.'

Mr. Mates: I will leave the interpreter of mandarin to draw his own conclusions.

The whole UK-US relationship must obviously be examined too. There are reams of papers that explain and reveal how the two were interacting in that relationship and how that led to certain decisions being taken that, if they had been presented differently, might have been taken differently. There were crucial reports of the key moments in the decision-making process. First, there was the meeting between the Prime Minister and the President in Texas, at President Bush's ranch in Crawford. Then there was the meeting between the Prime Minister and the President in Washington from which Sir Christopher Meyer was excluded. Then there is a series of documents written by Sir David Manning, the Prime Minister's adviser on overseas and foreign policy. Those documents are crucial to understanding the way in which all the decisions were made. The press have speculated about them – sometimes correctly, sometimes incorrectly – and some have been leaked. Having seen them all, I know how crucial those documents are for the Chilcot inquiry to be able to do its job properly.

Last of all, if ever there was a war in which politics – that is, in the decision to go to war, not the war itself – played such a major part, it was this one, given the political decisions taken here and in the United States. As I speak these words, I can hear colleagues saying, 'He would say this, wouldn't he?' Why are there no politicians on the committee? That point was made very well by my right hon. Friend the Member for Chingford and Woodford Green (Mr. Duncan Smith) and the hon. and learned Member for Medway, as well as by others, from all round the House. The reason the Prime Minister gave us was this:

> 'the membership of the committee will consist entirely of non-partisan public figures acknowledged to be experts and leaders … There will be no representatives of political parties from either side of this House.' – [*Official Report*, 15 June 2009; Vol. 494, c. 24.]

David Davis MP: I commend my right hon. Friend on making an astonishingly informative speech. To reinforce his comment about politicians being involved, everything that he has described is mirrored in similar failures – constitutional, structural, governmental and decision-making failures – in the United States. They have come out recently because of the torture issue and how legality was bypassed, so it is doubly important that politicians should be involved …

George Galloway MP: … The Prime Minister's initial prospectus for this inquiry proved that the Government just do not get it. When, in 2005, I was elected as the first left-of-Labour Member of Parliament in England for 60 years, I was elected because of Iraq. The Labour party's membership has halved because of Iraq. Millions of Labour voters have left them and new parties – some of the left and some of the right – are proliferating and strengthening, in substantial part because of Iraq. That has happened not directly, but indirectly because of the poison that the Iraq question has caused to pulse around the British body politic. The lack of credibility of the British political class has also been the result of Iraq.

The Government still do not get it. If they did, they would have used this opportunity for a grand catharsis, to turn the page and finally leave Blairism behind and call for the kind of inquiry that has been repeatedly demanded in the House this evening.

… Some of us say, to reverse Talleyrand, that this was worse than a blunder; it was a crime. If the inquiry is to mean anything, it will need to be able not only to apportion blame but, if blame is apportioned, to signal what legal avenues should be pursued. I know that we do not like that sort of thing in this country – things are usually swept under the carpet and finessed – but this is new territory. Events such as the expenses scandal have left the country seeing our House with such odium, and this country's political class so naked, that the old ways will not do. If the inquiry finds people guilty of misleading Parliament, the Queen, the armed forces and the public, they will have to be held accountable. There will have to be a trial, which will have to be held under oath, and that will lead to punishment if there are convictions at the end – nothing less will do …

Alan Simpson MP: … I remind the House of some of the inconvenient elements that were already in place in the run-up to the war in 2003. I pay tribute to many of my hon. Friends, some of whom are in their places, who at that time formed Labour Against the War. It was to demonstrate in the Chamber that there was not a consensus in the Labour party that endorsed the country being bounced into an illegal and immoral war.

It was under the auspices of Labour Against the War that we brought into the Palace of Westminster several of the key international players who ought to have informed our debate. Dominique de Villepin was here, and he set out the French perspective. Scott Ritter, a former head of the United Nations Special Commission weapons inspectors, came here and set out what the inspectors already knew about the destruction of both Iraq's capabilities and its potential to deliver weapons of mass destruction. He gave UNSCOM's evidence to Members who were interested. Denis Halliday, the UN humanitarian co-ordinator, came and told us what a devastating mess we were already making in Iraq and how disastrous it would be to compound that error.

On the eve of the publication of the Government's dodgy dossier, those of us who had the temerity to do so produced a counter-dossier, which was Labour Against the War's case against the war in Iraq. It set out the degree of international evidence available that contradicted all the claims that were coming out of Downing street. The inquiry therefore needs to address how, in the face of that evidence, this House could be bounced into a war of choice.

A number of hon. Members have referred to the importance of the availability of the legal advice at the time. However, it is not enough to have access to the legal advice; it is also important that the memorandums and notes of meetings should be available. Two of those memorandums that have already been widely leaked have been mentioned. My hon. and learned Friend the Member for Medway (Mr. Marshall-Andrews) referred to the secret Downing street memo produced on 23 July 2002 by David Manning and Matthew Rycroft, the Prime Minister's foreign policy adviser at the time. My hon. and learned Friend cited the comments by the head of MI6 about the need to fix the facts around the policy. However, I was far more interested in the comments made by elected Members of this House at the meeting described in that memorandum.

The then Foreign Secretary, for instance, said:

'It seemed clear that Bush had made up his mind to take military action, even if the timing was not yet decided. But the case was thin.'

In an attempt to be helpful, the then Defence Secretary said that

'if the Prime Minister wanted UK military involvement, he would need to decide this early.'

Even at that time, however, the Attorney-General said that

'the desire for regime change was not a legal base for military action'.

In conclusion, however, the then Prime Minister said:

'If the political context were right, people would support regime change. The two key issues were whether the military plan worked and whether we had a political strategy to give it the space to work.'

For the Prime Minister, the question was not then, and perhaps never was, whether the war was legal. It was not then, and possibly never was, whether there were weapons of mass destruction. The question was: can we manufacture the case for a war, in order to con the country, the Cabinet and the Commons into endorsing that plan? That absence of legality and the cynical manipulation of a case for a war of choice must be the focus of the inquiry's work.

The second note relates to the meeting that took place in the Oval Office on 31 January 2003, to which the right hon. Member for East Hampshire (Mr. Mates) referred. He is right to question the absence from that meeting of both members of Cabinet and the UK ambassador to the US, because there were only three people at that meeting from the UK side: the Prime Minister, Jonathan Powell, his chief of staff, and Matthew Rycroft, the foreign policy aide who was the author of the memo. However, that memo said that

> 'the president and the prime minister acknowledged that no unconventional weapons had been found inside Iraq. Faced with the possibility of not finding any before the planned invasion, Mr. Bush talked about several ways to provoke a confrontation, including a proposal to paint a United States surveillance plane in the colors of the United Nations in hopes of drawing fire, or assassinating Mr. Hussein.'

That is the cynical pursuit of conditions under which it will be possible to manufacture a case for legally going to war when no legal basis for doing so exists.

The inquiry must address to what extent members of the Cabinet were ever informed of those discussions. It must address whether the Cabinet knew, for instance, that the then Prime Minister was planning a war of choice in Iraq nine months before it was fought; that his objective was regime change, not the removal of weapons of mass destruction; that he had agreed nine months in advance to fix intelligence and facts around the Bush policy; and that Britain, based on the Prime Minister's approval, was colluding with acts of provocation or assassination.

Those are all illegal acts …

Adam Price MP: … I remember when the then Prime Minister spoke at that Dispatch Box on that terrible day for our democracy. He referred to the UN inspectors' reports, which contained, he said, unanswered questions and

> '29 different areas in which the inspectors have been unable to obtain information'. – [*Official Report*, 18 March 2003; Vol. 401, c. 763.]

He used that terrible Rumsfeldian logic. Absence of evidence is not evidence of absence; the fact that there was no evidence of WMD did not mean that the WMD were not there. That was sufficient reason – justification – for the war.

I did not believe a word that the Prime Minister said, but many hon. Members believed that it was not possible for a serving Prime Minister to lie to the House and to the people. Because he is no longer a Member of the House, I no longer have to fear being ejected for saying what many people believe: we were misled and the House was misled on a matter so serious – life or death, peace or war. That is why it is our responsibility tonight to get to the heart of the matter, both the specifics of the Iraq war and how our democracy and our machinery of government were so terribly undermined. We have to establish the truth and ensure that that never happens again – and yes, if as a result of that the inquiry believes that it must attribute blame, it should be free to do so if there is individual culpability, as many of us believe.

There are three key issues that the inquiry must consider and which have been touched on by many hon. and right hon. Members. On the motivation for the war, I believe that WMD were the pretext. As we have heard, various minutes and the Downing street memos that have emerged subsequent to the Butler inquiry suggest clearly, as Wolfowitz said, that WMD were simply the bureaucratic rationale. The real reason lay elsewhere, and it was regime change all along.

On legality, the contribution made by the right hon. Member for East Hampshire (Mr. Mates) was fascinating and it chimes with what Philippe Sands said in his book, 'Lawless World': the Butler inquiry saw correspondence between Ministers that the Cabinet never saw and which raised serious doubts about the legality of the war, and indeed shared some doubts that Colin Powell had about its legality.

We now know that the legal advisers in the Foreign Ministry of the Dutch Government believed that

'the Netherlands would lose any case brought before the International Court of Justice'.

Interestingly, written on that memorandum were the words:

'Bury it well in the archives for future generations.'

Our memorandums will not be buried. We owe it to future generations to ensure that this does not happen again.

Will there be prima facie evidence? Will the inquiry conclude that there is evidence that the war was indeed unlawful? We must remember that in

November, Lord Bingham, former Lord Chief Justice and senior Law Lord of the United Kingdom, said that the Attorney-General's advice to the British Government contained

'no hard evidence',

that Iraq had defied UN resolutions

'in a manner justifying resort to force'

and that the invasion – the Iraq war – was

'a serious violation of international law and of the rule of law' in this country as well ...

I believe that if the inquiry concludes – as the senior Law Lord of the United Kingdom has concluded – that the war was indeed unlawful, the Government should voluntarily report themselves. They should report the Iraq war to the International Court of Justice for a declaratory opinion so that we can ensure that, for the avoidance of doubt, it is established in international law for future generations, and so that the hundreds of thousands of Iraqis and the 179 British servicemen and women who lost their lives will not have lost them in vain. We will then have established a core principle in our democracy: that those who lead us cannot mislead us and expect to get away with it ...

War Crimes III

The Downing Street Memo

Matthew Rycroft

We first published the Memo in Spokesman 87, and reprint it in full again now because of its centrality to the debate about how Britain went to war on Iraq. Bob Marshall-Andrews MP and Alan Simpson MP emphasise this in their contributions to the recent Parliamentary debate (see pages 15 to 25). A collection of related documents is available in The Dodgiest Dossier *(£4, www.spokesmanbooks.com). Matthew Rycroft and David Manning have been described as a 'Downing Street foreign policy aides'.*

This revealing memorandum about preparations for war on Iraq, dating from July 2002, was leaked to the press in the days before the 2005 General Election, when Tony Blair was re-elected for the second time. Under Gordon Brown's original proposals for the Chilcot Inquiry on Iraq, which specified a start time of Autumn 2002, the Downing Street Memo may have fallen outside the remit of the committee. However, the timescale was put back to 2001, following representations from the Opposition parties, according to William Hague.

* * *

SECRET AND STRICTLY PERSONAL – UK EYES ONLY

DAVID MANNING
From: Matthew Rycroft
Date: 23 July 2002
S 195 02

cc: Defence Secretary, Foreign Secretary, Attorney-General, Sir Richard Wilson, John Scarlett, Francis Richards, CDS, C, Jonathan Powell, Sally Morgan, Alastair Campbell

IRAQ: PRIME MINISTER'S MEETING, 23 JULY

Copy addressees and you met the Prime Minister on 23 July to discuss Iraq.

This record is extremely sensitive. No further copies should be made. It should be shown only to those with a genuine need to know its contents.

John Scarlett summarised the intelligence and latest JIC [Joint Intelligence Committee] assessment. Saddam's regime was tough and based on extreme fear. The only way to overthrow it was likely to be by massive military action. Saddam was worried and expected an attack, probably by air and land, but he was not convinced that it would be immediate or overwhelming. His regime expected their neighbours to line up with the US. Saddam knew that regular army morale was poor. Real support for Saddam among the public was probably narrowly based.

C reported on his recent talks in Washington. There was a perceptible shift in attitude. Military action was now seen as inevitable. Bush wanted to remove Saddam, through military action, justified by the conjunction of terrorism and WMD [Weapons of Mass Destruction]. But the intelligence and facts were being fixed around the policy. The NSC [National Security Council] had no patience with the UN route, and no enthusiasm for publishing material on the Iraqi regime's record. There was little discussion in Washington of the aftermath after military action.

CDS [Chief of the Defence Staff] said that military planners would brief CENTCOM on 1-2 August, Rumsfeld on 3 August and Bush on 4 August.

The two broad US options were:

(a) Generated Start. A slow build-up of 250,000 US troops, a short (72 hour) air campaign, then a move up to Baghdad from the south. Lead time of 90 days (30 days preparation plus 60 days deployment to Kuwait).

(b) Running Start. Use forces already in theatre (3 x 6,000), continuous air campaign, initiated by an Iraqi casus belli. Total lead time of 60 days with the air campaign beginning even earlier. A hazardous option.

The US saw the UK (and Kuwait) as essential, with basing in Diego Garcia and Cyprus critical for either option. Turkey and other Gulf states were also important, but less vital. The three main options for UK involvement were:

(i) Basing in Diego Garcia and Cyprus, plus three SF [Special Forces] squadrons.

(ii) As above, with maritime and air assets in addition.

(iii) As above, plus a land contribution of up to 40,000, perhaps with a discrete role in Northern Iraq entering from Turkey, tying down two Iraqi divisions.

The Defence Secretary said that the US had already begun "spikes of activity" to put pressure on the regime. No decisions had been taken, but he thought the most likely timing in US minds for military action to begin was January, with the timeline beginning 30 days before the US

Congressional elections.

The Foreign Secretary said he would discuss this with Colin Powell this week. It seemed clear that Bush had made up his mind to take military action, even if the timing was not yet decided. But the case was thin. Saddam was not threatening his neighbours, and his WMD capability was less than that of Libya, North Korea or Iran. We should work up a plan for an ultimatum to Saddam to allow back in the UN weapons inspectors. This would also help with the legal justification for the use of force.

The Attorney-General said that the desire for regime change was not a legal base for military action. There were three possible legal bases: self-defence, humanitarian intervention, or UNSC [United Nations Security Council] authorisation. The first and second could not be the base in this case. Relying on UNSCR 1205 of three years ago would be difficult. The situation might of course change.

The Prime Minister said that it would make a big difference politically and legally if Saddam refused to allow in the UN inspectors. Regime change and WMD were linked in the sense that it was the regime that was producing the WMD. There were different strategies for dealing with Libya and Iran. If the political context were right, people would support regime change. The two key issues were whether the military plan worked and whether we had the political strategy to give the military plan the space to work.

On the first, CDS said that we did not know yet if the US battleplan was workable. The military were continuing to ask lots of questions.

For instance, what were the consequences, if Saddam used WMD on day one, or if Baghdad did not collapse and urban warfighting began? You said that Saddam could also use his WMD on Kuwait. Or on Israel, added the Defence Secretary.

The Foreign Secretary thought the US would not go ahead with a military plan unless convinced that it was a winning strategy. On this, US and UK interests converged. But on the political strategy, there could be US/UK differences. Despite US resistance, we should explore discreetly the ultimatum. Saddam would continue to play hard-ball with the UN.

John Scarlett assessed that Saddam would allow the inspectors back in only when he thought the threat of military action was real.

The Defence Secretary said that if the Prime Minister wanted UK military involvement, he would need to decide this early. He cautioned that many in the US did not think it worth going down the ultimatum route. It would be important for the Prime Minister to set out the political context to Bush.

Conclusions:

(a) We should work on the assumption that the UK would take part in any military action. But we needed a fuller picture of US planning before we could take any firm decisions. CDS should tell the US military that we were considering a range of options.

(b) The Prime Minister would revert on the question of whether funds could be spent in preparation for this operation.

(c) CDS would send the Prime Minister full details of the proposed military campaign and possible UK contributions by the end of the week.

(d) The Foreign Secretary would send the Prime Minister the background on the UN inspectors, and discreetly work up the ultimatum to Saddam.He would also send the Prime Minister advice on the positions of countries in the region especially Turkey, and of the key EU member states.

(e) John Scarlett would send the Prime Minister a full intelligence update.

(f) We must not ignore the legal issues: the Attorney-General would consider legal advice with FCO/MOD legal advisers.

(I have written separately to commission this follow-up work.)

War Crimes IV

An Indictment of Tony Blair

E. W. Thomas

Mr Brown's Inquiry will not 'apportion blame or consider issues of civil or criminal liability'. However, one lawyer has sought to uphold the law. He has made his own 'survey for which it could be reasonably expected Tony Blair should be accountable'. The Rt Hon E.W.Thomas QC PC, Retired Judge of the Court of Appeal of New Zealand, and Acting Judge of the Supreme Court of New Zealand, has prepared 'An indictment of Tony Blair and the failure of the political process' (see War Crimes, Spokesman 95*). 'The following list is not a legal indictment, as such,' he says. 'It makes no rigid distinction between political morality, legality or, even, political misjudgement.'*

1. In supporting the war in Iraq, the Prime Minister allied the United Kingdom, and the Labour Government and Labour Party, with the neo-conservative and ideologically driven administration in the United States. It was beholden on him to assert greater independence and recognize that the policies of the Bush administration were both unrealistic and simplistic.

2. In particular, he effectively endorsed the Bush administration's ill-conceived war model as an appropriate response to the threat of terrorism.

3. The Prime Minister unilaterally committed the United Kingdom to support the United States invasion of Iraq without obtaining the timely sanction of his Cabinet or Parliament. Such sanction as was later obtained was obtained through manipulation and political deceit.

4. In particular, he manipulated the intelligence of the security agencies and was deliberately deceptive when he initially shifted from the claim that Iraq had the potential to develop weapons of mass destruction to the claim that Iraq actually possessed those weapons. Further, his uncritical acceptance of the faith-based intelligence of the Bush administration was inexcusable.

5. In respect of the dossier of September 2002, the Prime Minister deliberately misrepresented the intelligence by omitting the reservations, qualifications and caveats in that intelligence.

6. In particular, his claim that Iraq could launch missiles carrying weapons of mass destruction within 45 minutes was a serious misrepresentation which the Prime Minister must have known was false, or which he

came to know was false before he ceased making that claim.

7. The Prime Minister misrepresented, and must have known that he was misrepresenting, the advice which he received from the Attorney-General as to the legality of the war against Iraq. It is impossible to accept that the Prime Minister did not know that there was no sound legal basis for the war. Hence it is difficult to escape the conclusion that he was guilty of the crime of aggression.

8. The Prime Minister has been less than emphatic and, indeed, benignly forgiving, in his rejection of the use of torture, principally because of his knowledge of, and effective complicity in, the United States' practice of extraordinary renditions and his insistence on deporting non-nationals to countries where there is a real risk they will be tortured.

9. The Prime Minister, at the very least, condoned the ideological aim of the Bush administration to establish a *laissez-faire* economy which was self-evidently unreal, would have resulted in the exploitation of Iraq's people and resources by corporate America, and would eventually have led to civil instability.

10. The Prime Minister must accept responsibility for the passage of legislation which constitutes an erosion of fundamental human rights unprecedented in recent British history.

11. The Prime Minister has impaired the democratic process in manipulating Cabinet and Parliament, and he must accept responsibility for the unprecedented level of 'spin' used in promoting the war against Iraq. The spin was nothing short of propaganda.

12. In the course of preparing for and supporting the war in Iraq, the Prime Minister displayed an unacceptable disdain for the democratic process, the rule of law and fundamental human rights and civil liberties. The rules of international law have fared no better.

The Banks – Too Big To Fail

Michael Barratt Brown

Michael Barratt Brown is the founding Principal of Northern College in Yorkshire. His book Global Crisis *treats extensively the problem of redistribution of wealth (Spokesman Books, £9).*

Government ministers, bankers, businessmen and women and the media have begun to talk hopefully about the ending of the current recession, and 'the green shoots' of recovery already showing when economic growth will start again. Ludicrous as such a suggestion must be of further growth of the kind we have been enjoying being sustained within the limits of the planet's capacity, talk of an early recovery is a profound misjudgement of the real situation. This has been clearly revealed in two recent authoritative publications. The first on 'Green shoots or yellow reeds' – mainly about the United States economy – appeared in Nouriel Roubini's *Global EconoMonitor* for May 19th. The second – mainly about the UK banks – was written by John Lanchester, entitled 'It's Finished', taking up eight full pages of the *London Review of Books* issue of May 28th. Any reader of these two papers must be left with profound doubts about our economic future.

Despite the failure of earlier promises of recovery by mid-2009, a research group at Goldman Sachs bank in the United States was still predicting, in March 2009, an early bottoming out of the recession on the basis of four improving trends – employment, retail sales, industrial production, and housing conditions. In each of these areas Roubini shows that improvement is quite simply not occurring. Unemployment is likely to rise to 11% by 2011. Retail sales and consumption have been falling sharply since April, and are hardly likely to recover as employment falls and savings have to be rebuilt. Industrial production, of motor vehicles, for example, is still declining as home demand, especially in China, shows no sign of replacing falling exports. Housing starts and building permits are still falling with a huge inventory of unsold homes and unpaid mortgages. This is the immediate picture for the United States, but worldwide and in the longer term the picture, which Roubini paints, is no brighter.

The risks and vulnerabilities

Roubini identifies ten risks and vulnerabilities for the world economy in the medium-term future. The first, and the one that influences all the others, is that the cause of the crisis has been misunderstood. Wrong remedies have been applied. Instead of recognising excessive over-borrowing and over-spending as the problem, it has been treated as a crisis of financial confidence. Debts have been transferred by Government intervention from private banks and households to the state. But they still hang over the whole world economy.

The second is that the response to debt by households and businesses and by the state is to reduce spending and increase savings. But this only has the effect of deepening the depression. The debt overhang has not been reduced, so that spending, preferably on investment goods, can be resumed and the productive cycle restarted.

The third is that, with banks weighed down by the burden of bad loans and toxic securities and by trillions of expected losses, and with hedge funds closing, the current credit crunch is likely to persist for a long time. Again, the cycle of demand led production is held back.

The fourth is that the big corporations – the motor car industry as a prime example – are equally under financial stress, with outstanding debts and vast excess capacity, partly as a result of massive over investment by China.

The fifth is that the socialisation of private losses and debts implies a sharp rise in public debt, which will rise from about 40% of gross domestic product (national income) to 80%. Interest rates are bound to rise, crowding out private spending.

The sixth is that government monetisation of fiscal deficits must lead to inflationary pressures and an end to the years of price stability, which have been sustaining growth, misplaced as it has been in excessive consumption at the expense of investment.

The seventh is that rising unemployment is likely to continue beyond 2010, with the threat for the United States and Europe of over two billion more Chinese and Indians in the global labour force.

The eighth is that the economic balance will end whereby up till now countries running deficits, consuming more than they produced – the

United States, United Kingdom, Australia and New Zealand – have been absorbing the surplus output of countries producing more than they consume – China, Japan, East Asia, and also Germany, unless they begin to expand their internal consumption. Such a change in consumption patterns, with a switch to more investment, is likely to take many years.

The ninth is that mistaken government policies in future – protection of markets for goods and capital, heavy taxation and state intervention – could easily result in sub-par development.

'It's pretty clear by now that this is the worst financial crisis, economic crisis and recession since the Great Depression. A number of us were worrying about it a while ago. At this point it's becoming conventional wisdom.

The good news is probably that six months ago there was a risk of a near depression, but we have seen very aggressive actions by US policymakers, and around the world. I think the policymakers finally looked into the abyss: they saw that the economy was contracting at a rate of 6 per cent-plus in the United States and around the world, and decided to use almost all of the weapons in their arsenals. Because of that I think that the risk of a near depression has been somewhat reduced. I don't think that there is zero probability, but most likely we are not going to end up in a near depression.

However, the consensus is now becoming optimistic again and says that we are going to go from minus 6 per cent growth to positive growth in the second half of this year, meaning that the recession is going to be over by June. By the fourth quarter of 2009, the consensus estimates that growth is going to be positive, by 2 per cent, and next year more than 2 per cent. Now, compared to that new consensus among macro forecasters, who got it wrong in the past, my views are much more bearish.

I would agree that the rate of economic contraction is slowing down. But we're still contracting at a pretty fast rate. I see the economy contracting all the way through the end of the year, going from minus 6 to minus 2, not plus 2. And next year the growth of the economy is going to be very slow, 0.5 per cent as opposed to the 2 per cent-plus predicted by the consensus. Also, the unemployment rate this year is going to be above 10 per cent, and is likely to be close to 11 per cent next year. Thus, next year is still going to feel like a recession, even if we're technically out of the recession.

The outlook for Europe and Japan, both this year and next year, is even worse. Most of the advanced economies are going to do worse than the United States for a number of reasons, including structural factors in Japan and weak policy response in the case of the Eurozone.

The problems of the financial system are severe. Many banks are still insolvent. If you don't want to end up like Japan with zombie banks, it's better

The tenth is that, in addition to all the risks already described, a long period of recession will lead to the loss of skills and innovation and, though Roubini does not mention this, the necessary adaptation of consumption and production to the results of climate change.

After presenting this list of risks and vulnerabilities likely to delay global economic recovery, Roubini warns that a temporary recovery might be followed by a further recession – what is called a W-shaped recession, not just his expected U-shaped one. This could be caused by commodity

---

… to do what Sweden did: take over the insolvent banks, clean them up, separate good and bad assets, and sell them back in short order to the private sector.

Now, on the question of policy responses, there is no inconsistency between monetary easing and fiscal easing. Both of them should be stimulating demand, and the monetary easing should be leading also to restoration of credit. Of course, in a situation in which the economy is suffering not just from a lack of liquidity but also problems of solvency and a lack of credit, traditional monetary policy doesn't work as well. You also have to take unconventional monetary actions, and you have to fix the banks. And we need a fiscal stimulus because every component of our economy is sharply falling: consumption, residential investment, non-residential construction, capital spending, inventories, exports. The only thing that can go up and sustain the economy for the time being is the fiscal spending of the government.

However, fiscal policy cannot resolve problems of credit, and it is not without cost. Over the next few years it's going to add about $9 trillion to the US public debt. Niall Ferguson said it's the end of the age of leverage. It's not really. There is not de-leveraging. We have all the liabilities of the household sector, of the banks and financial institutions, of the corporate sectors; and now we've decided to socialize these bad debts and to put them on the balance sheet of the government. That's why the public debt is rising. Instead, when you have an excessive debt problem, you have to convert such debt into equity. That's what you do with corporate restructuring–it converts unsecured debt into equity. That's what you should do with the banks: induce the unsecured creditors to convert their claims into equity. You could do the same thing with the housing market. But we're not doing the debt-into-equity conversion. What we're doing is piling public debt on top of private debt to socialize the losses; and at some point the back of some government's balance sheet is going to break, and if that happens, it's going to be a disaster. So we need fiscal stimulus in the short run, but we have to worry about the long-run fiscal sustainability, too.'

Nouriel Roubini, New York Review of Books, 11 June 2009

price increases, government tax increases, and/or inflationary pressures.

The dangers of corporate size

The sheer size of banks and industrial corporations has exacerbated the problems of financial and economic instability. John Lanchester in his article supplies some history of this growth in corporate size. The Royal Bank of Scotland (RBS), now since its takeover of NatWest, by asset size the biggest company in the world (with the ex-chief executive Sir Fred Goodwin enjoying one of the largest pensions), is the chief object of Lanchester's very detailed company accounts examination. Assets of RBS in 2007 are shown as amounting to £1.9 trillion when the whole UK gross domestic product amounted to £1.672 trillion. RBS as a bank arose from the failed Scottish Darien (Panama) trading speculation in 1695, the subsequent massive Scottish losses and the bail-out of compensation organised as part of the Act of Union of England and Scotland in 1707. But RBS is not the only giant of British banking. In the United States there are still many banks in the different states, though the failed Lehmans and the American Insurance Group (AIG) were very large. By contrast, there are now just four joint stock banks in Britain's high streets – RBS-NatWest (once National Provincial), Lloyds-HBOS (once Halifax Building Society and the Bank of Scotland), Barclays and Midland-HSBC (Hong Kong and Shanghai Bank of China). All had manufacturing and trading origins with overseas Empire connexions. The Co-operative Bank and Nationwide are mutual societies owned by their depositors.

What, it may well be asked, has been the advantage of size that has led to this succession of bank mergers and takeovers? It is not difficult to understand in terms of monopoly positions and economies of scale why size has been increasing in manufacturing, mining and retailing, but why in banking? Lanchester offers a convincing explanation. Shareholder value, that is the value of shares on the Stock Exchange, does not depend so much on productive efficiency as on confidence in survival. Size is reassuring and great size means 'too big to fail'. State support can be relied upon to rescue failing banks, and this has proved only too true in the current crisis. But the next question is why the tell-tale signs of over spending, over lending and 'toxic assets' did not show up in the banks' accounts. Sir Fred Goodwin, in 2008, promised his RBS share holders that great caution had been exercised to avoid any failure like that of Northern Rock, yet within a few days RBS had to be bailed out by the government. Lanchester's detailed examination of RBS's accounts (in itself a beautiful model for a business school exercise in the study of company balance sheets) shows in the relevant footnotes that mortgage-backed securities rose in 2007 to £68.302 billion from £32.19 billion in the previous year. Derivatives insurances had risen to £377 billions of assets, compared to £116 billions the year before. Surely, he suggests, these were warning signs that were not picked up, but resulted in the meltdown of confidence that forced government to step in.

With the exception of Barclays and HSBC, the largest British banks were all in serious trouble in 2008.

> 'The fact is,' Lanchester concludes, 'that nobody knows which banks are solvent. Because banks are crucial to the creation and operation of credit, a bank crisis leads directly to a credit crunch. It is also the reason the huge amounts of money being pumped into the banking sector by governments are tending not to do the thing they are supposed to do, i.e. restart lending to businesses and consumers. That's because – and here we can have that very rare thing, a brief moment of sympathy for the banksters – the banks are being given two totally incompatible goals. One is to rebuild their balance sheet and recapitalise themselves so that they're no longer at risk of being broke. The second is to keep lending money. They're being told to save and keep spending at the same time.'

Banks which are kept in business when they are insolvent become what may be called 'zombie banks'. Their managers need either to be forced to admit what their assets are worth. If they are proved to be insolvent, then they need either to be nationalised or broken up into viable bits and put on sale on the market. No one in government or in the banking system wants to do either. So the government pumps huge sums of money into the banks to keep them solvent, at least £500 billion in the United Kingdom and much more in the United States. This does not rid the system of its toxic assets. It is being assumed that there is a crisis of liquidity that can be met with funds, and not a crisis of solvency, which needs radical action.

Why the banks are not being nationalised

In the end, short of nationalisation, what happened? The debts and losses of RBS amounted to at least £100 billions, plus the unaccounted debts of companies taken over by RBS. Similar enormous sums were involved in the losses of most of the other UK banks, and even larger sums in the United States. Government action taken is described as 'bailing out'. This means a number of quite different actions by governments, ranging from the supply of capital and loans to various forms of insurance against future losses. The most common of the latter is an asset protection scheme called a Credit Default Swap or CDS. This, rather than capital provision or nationalisation, has been the main instrument employed both by US and British governments, to bail out the bankrupt companies. The sums involved are enormous, and their impact on future economic development very serious, as Roubini has shown. It is not being suggested here that nationalisation of the banks would be a simple solution to the problem, but it is interesting to note that Lanchester lists four major reasons for governments' reluctance to take over the banks.

Once upon a time, in the 1930s, Harold Macmillan, in his address to the electors of Stockton, proposed as the National Conservative candidate, a number of forms of nationalisation – railways and mines – but also the Bank of England and the joint stock banks. It so happened that Macmillan was the Treasurer of the 1930s think-tank, the Next Five Years Group, of which my father was the Secretary. As a very young student, I was rather honoured to be shown Macmillan's address and asked for my comments. I rather cheekily replied that I understood the 'National' bit , but where was the 'Conservative' bit? Macmillan's reply was immediate, 'It depends, young man, on what you intend to conserve'. I had to ask my father what Harold meant, and was told 'the capitalist system'. It seems unlikely, some 75 years later, that the same answer could be given with the same confidence in the current crisis. But the reasons for governments' continued reluctance to nationalise are perhaps stronger than ever.

These are the arguments quoted by Lanchester as grounds for this reluctance:

1. Governments would be bad at the job. 'What?' asks Lanchester, 'worse than the bankers who broke capitalism?'
2. Every banking decision made by governments would be blamed on the government – refused mortgages, refused loans to business. These would all carry a high political cost.
3. Paying off the banks' debts is going to mean tax rises, a near freeze on government expenditure, public sector job cuts, school and hospital building delayed, rising unemployment in the private sector, higher rates of inflation, reduced imports. Governments would think it better to blame the bankers than take the blame on themselves.
4. Above all, abandoning the whole Washington-London 'Anglo-Saxon' capitalist model and admitting that it had failed would be acutely embarrassing, as well as political suicide. So it won't happen.

As events have unfolded since the financial crisis broke in 2007, media interest has been directed at the obscene bonuses and pensions of the bankers and then at the fiddled expense accounts of Members of Parliament. It might almost seem as if these were intended to divert attention from massive malfeasance of the banking system, and government involvement in it. Combined with these events, there is the desperately underestimated impact of climate change. The fact is that the whole situation puts into question the very survival of our parliamentary capitalist system. As popular anger grows, it can hardly be assuaged by voting within the current political structures for the candidates of a plethora of dissident political parties. Something of a revolution in political thought and action will emerge, as systemic political and economic failure, and the very real threats to the survival of the planet and of human existence on it, come to be recognised.

Banking and Finance
What Labour Forgot

J. E. Mortimer

Jim Mortimer was General Secretary of the Labour Party from 1982 to 1985. He recently alerted us to the contemporary relevance of the Labour Party's statement on Banking and Finance, which was originally agreed in 1976. It has just been republished by Socialist Renewal under the title Labour's forgotten statement on Banking and Finance *(price £3 from www.spokesmanbooks.com). Here we reprint Jim Mortimer's new introduction together with a short excerpt from the conclusion to the statement.*

In the discussion within the labour movement and the press about the current failings of the financial system, the 'credit crunch' and the consequential rise in unemployment, little, if any, attention has been given to a statement entitled 'Banking and Finance', prepared by the National Executive Committee of the Labour Party and then presented to and accepted by the 1976 annual conference of the Party.

The report saw the operation of Britain's financial system within the wider context of the problems of the economy. How right they were! At the heart of these problems was the need to increase industrial investment. This need, said the Labour Party report, was 'too important to be left to businessmen and financiers alone'. The report called for a doubling of the rate of manufacturing investment over the next decade. Manufacturing, it said, had 'grown anaemic and needed a major transformation'.

The Labour Party's statement argued that the funds to pay for such a massive expansion of manufacturing investment could not come solely from ploughed back profits or even from a strengthened National Enterprise Board. A larger proportion of long-term funds would have to come from outside sources such as banks and other financial institutions. Hence it was essential to examine the flow of funds to ensure that industry had the necessary degree of support.

This warning from the Labour Party was in large measure disregarded. Manufacturing continued to shrink and soothing words were used about the growth of financial services and the services sector. The Labour Party made proposals for the extension of social ownership and fundamental changes in policy.

In subsequent years, the housing policy, associated above all with Mrs Thatcher, worsened the situation. Council house building for rent declined at a steep rate. All the emphasis was on the growth of home ownership, with ever-increasing debt. The assumption was that the debt would be met by the ever-increasing prices of property, providing so-called 'gains in capital equity'. When the bubble burst, we all became familiar with the term 'sub-prime mortgages'. The downturn started in the United States and spread rapidly to many other countries, including Britain.

Unfortunately, the Labour Party's 1976 statement on 'Banking and Finance' was not adopted as a guide by New Labour when it was elected with an overwhelming majority in 1997. There is a lesson in this experience.

* * *

The main conclusions of the Labour Party's 1976 statement on Banking and Finance are summarised in this excerpt.

'For too long the financial system has been able to shelter behind a mystique of its own creation. That mystique has finally been punctured by the extent of the threat to confidence and to people's savings from a series of failures which now compel serious questioning of the operations of the financial system. The "difficulties" experienced by second mortgage specialists Cedar Holdings and First National Finance; by finance houses Moorgate Mercantile, United Dominion Trust, Mercantile Credit and Lombard North Central; by London and County Securities, Western Credit, Keyser Ullman and Cannon Street Investments; the failures of Vehicle and General, Bastion Insurance, London Indemnity and General Insurance, and Nation Life Insurance; and the current problems of merchant bankers Edward Bates all suggest that the 1967 companies Act, the 1973 Insurance Companies Amendment Act etc. were nowhere near tough enough to safeguard the public. We must now recognise the commanding heights of the economy for what they are, and acknowledge that a major publicly-owned stake in banking and insurance is an essential condition for a viable economic strategy and for sustained recovery.

Our experience of industry and the financial system teaches us that we would be unwise either to wait upon their lead, or to passively accept the pace they adopt or to blindly follow in the direction they set. Accordingly this Statement proposes:

● A publicly-controlled Investment Reserve Fund Scheme to encourage firms to invest, as suggested in our 1975 Statement "Labour and Industry".

● Integration of the existing publicly-owned sections of the financial system by combining the Giro and National Savings Movement.

● A major publicly-owned stake in the financial system comprising the top seven insurance companies, (sufficient to account for 50 per cent of total premium income) a merchant bank and the four major private clearing banks, whose separate identities, services to customers and responsibilities to staff would be maintained.

● Reform of the Bank of England so that it ceases to be the spokesman for the private sector financial institutions and takes on responsibility for the investment fund scheme, for publicly-owned banking and insurance, and for co-ordinating and planning the provision of finance to industry.

It is essential that all sections of the Labour Movement, especially the unions representing banking and insurance staff, give voice to their feelings on these issues. The spokesmen of financial interests are already congratulating themselves on having survived the collapse of the property boom and its aftermath, conveniently forgetting the City's original escape into unreality. For 25 years the Doctrine of the Unripe Time has been used as an excuse for refusing to grasp the nettle. The lack of any outright commitment in Labour's October 1974 Manifesto other than "to ensure that banking and insurance make a better contribution to the national economy" need not prevent the Annual Conference from adding to the Party's official policy Programme. In doing so Conference should be aware of the extensive influence of bankers and financiers anxious to preserve the 'status quo', and their own privileged place within it, by claims that despite the evidence, all is for the best in the best of all possible financial worlds.'

European Elections – What Happened

Henry McCubbin

Henry McCubbin was a Member of the European Parliament from 1989 to 1994. He is a regular contributor to Scottish Left Review, *to whom we make grateful acknowledgements.*

The 2009 European elections must surely make Europe's socialist parties realise that triangulation with capitalist forces leads to nothing less than political strangulation. The pathetic state of the British Labour Party is the most telling. The distribution of support is clear from the table below. The party has fallen to third place behind, of all things, UKIP.

UK Total MEP Seats

Party	Votes %	+/- %	MEPs Total	+/-
CON	27.7	1.0	*26	1
UKIP	16.5	0.3	13	1
LAB	15.7	-6.9	13	-5
LD	13.7	-1.2	11	1
GRN	8.6	2.4	2	0
BNP	6.2	1.3	2	2
SNP	2.1	0.7	2	0
PC	0.8	-0.1	1	0
OTH	8.5	2.4	0	0
SF	–	–	1	0
DUP	–	–	1	0

72 of 72 seats declared. Vote share figures exclude Northern Ireland as it has a separate electoral system to the rest of the UK. *Includes Ulster Conservatives and Unionists – New Force (UCUNF MEP) elected in Northern Ireland.

Labour's precipitate decline has been on its way from before the hopeless Jack Straw changed the voting system in such a way as to concentrate power over candidate selection to the centre. This is a policy which is the only discernably consistent one in the numerous constitutional tweaks brought in under New Labour. The cliff-like decline in support only has its comparison with the decline of the economy under Gordon Brown, and is shown below in election on election series.

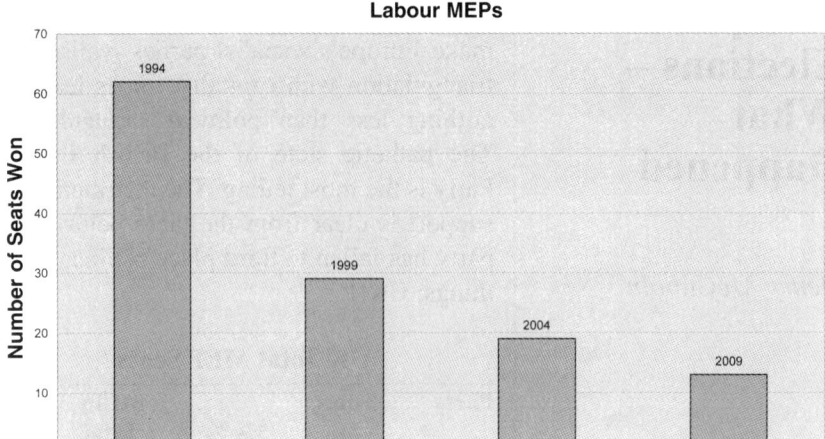

Labour MEPs

Labour's contribution to the socialist struggle has been a negative one with its instructions to its MEPs, through the despicable privatiser 'Postman' Pat McFadden, to attack workers' rights, whether so-called 'posted' workers or all workers through their blocking tactics over working time. In fact the only positive contribution they made was to reduce the number of MEPs to send to the European Parliament. You could discover Dutch liberals with a better left voting record than Labour MEPs such as Michael Cashman.

What is now clear is that the European People's Party (EPP) conservative alliance has reinforced its position in the European Parliament, and will clearly be the dominant group, although their total number of MEPs has been reduced, and their votes merely stabilised in comparison to 2004. Right wing leaders in power have, however, been confirmed as the first political force, such as Sarkozy and Tony Blair's friend Berlusconi.

The big losers were undoubtedly the socialists, who not only diminished their delegation, but also keep widening the distance in numbers of representatives between themselves and the conservatives. Additionally, they lost their positions at the national level in several countries, including the United Kingdom, where they are the governing party.

Liberals roughly kept their parliamentary representation, losing only 2 MEPs. They have approached the socialists in terms of parliamentary balance, as the latter shed 20 seats, five of who were formerly UK Labour.

The greens were the only group to raise their representation significantly (41 to 54 seats, more than 30%), while the GUE-NGL group, where the European Left (EL) members are represented, diminished from 37 to 35 MEPs. The GUE lost all representation from Italy where the left broke into small fractions and won nothing. We need only to look at the left's scattered support in Scotland to see that such behaviour is not nation specific.

However, beyond the general picture, there were mixed messages from the electorate around Europe. For example, in Portugal the Left Bloc (EL member) and the Communist Party had altogether more than 21% of votes (10.7% both) and Bloc significantly tripled its representation, now having three elected MEPs. In Germany, Die Link elected one more MEP, and in France the Front de Gauche elected two more. In Cyprus, AKEL (EL observer party) kept its strong position, only a few decimals behind the conservatives, with 34% of votes. Elsewhere in Europe other smaller progressive and left parties had positive results.

Greece did provide some respite in that the left, including PASOK, overtook the right. We can safely assume that the social turmoil last winter in Athens, where the left sided with the young demonstrators, may have contributed to this situation. In general, however, the results for the left, together with the socialists' results, and the fact that the latter are in power in several countries implementing contested policies, such as Portugal and Spain (where the right wing won), is a reminder about the challenges and difficult tasks for the left to build and publicly deliver an alternative political programme, recognizable as such by the electorate.

The wide and empty electoral space presented in these elections to the alternative left and those of progressive social protest, which has been created by the socialist parties and the failure of the dominant neoliberal model of development, therefore remained unoccupied by radical thinking from any sort of unified political movement of the European left or, in many cases, from the nation state left political field. Overall, and even including the results of the greens (as in the United Kingdom, and especially in France, where the greens more than doubled their result), it was mainly the right wing that gained from dissatisfaction across the European Union. This fact must not be exaggerated, since it was also accompanied by a general stabilization of voting compared to 2004. More than that, for instance in Portugal, the winning right party had a result not far from its historical lowest level.

On the other hand, the increase of conservative support was also worryingly linked to the right wing extremists in some countries. This is a particular danger for democracy and another challenge to democratic forces willing to protest constructively, attracting votes and building alternatives. The European Left alerted us to this problem in its electoral platform, characterized not only by the general crisis, but also by deep dissatisfaction and mistrust in politicians and their lack of ethics. This is patently clear in the United Kingdom with the scandals about parliamentarians' private expenses paid with public money.

Seats by political group in each Member State (provisional 11 June 2009)

	EPP	PES	ALDE	UEN	GREENS/ EFA	GUE/ NGL	IND/ DEM	Others	Total
BE	6	5	5	0	3	0	0	3	22
BG	6	4	5	0	0	0	0	2	17
CZ	2	7	0	0	0	4	0	9	22
DK	1	4	3	2	2	1	0	0	13
DE	42	23	12	0	14	8	0	0	99
EE	1	1	3	0	0	0	0	1	6
IE	4	3	1	3	0	0	0	1	12
EL	8	8	0	0	1	3	2	0	22
ES	23	21	2	0	2	1	0	1	50
FR	29	14	6	0	14	4	1	4	72
IT	35	0	7	9	0	0	0	21	72
CY	2	1	0	0	0	2	0	1	6
LV	1	0	1	3	1	0	0	2	8
LT	4	3	2	2	0	0	0	1	12
LU	3	1	1	0	1	0	0	0	6
HU	15	4	0	0	0	0	0	3	22
MT	2	3	0	0	0	0	0	0	5
NL	5	3	6	0	3	2	2	4	25
AT	6	4	0	0	2	0	0	5	17
PL	28	7	0	15	0	0	0	0	50
PT	10	7	0	0	0	5	0	0	22
RO	13	11	5	0	1	0	0	3	33
SI	3	2	2	0	0	0	0	0	7
SK	6	5	0	1	0	0	0	1	13
FI	4	2	4	0	2	0	0	1	13
SE	5	5	4	0	2	1	0	1	18
UK	0	13	11	0	5	1	13	29	72
EU total	264	161	80	35	53	32	18	93	736

- EPP : Group of the European People's Party (Christian Democrats)
- PES : Socialist Group in the European Parliament
- ALDE : Group of the Alliance of Liberals and Democrats for Europe
- UEN : Union for Europe of the Nations Group
- GREENS/ EFA : Group of the Greens / European Free Alliance
- GUE/ NGL : Confederal Group of the European United Left - Nordic Green Left
- IND/ DEM : Independence/Democracy Group
- Others : Others

Without prejudice to the composition of the European Parliament at the inaugural session on 14 July 2009

My A-Bomb Biography

James Kirkup

James Kirkup died in Andorra in May 2009, aged 91, writing poems to the end. He wrote these prefatory remarks to No More Hiroshimas, *his volume of poems published by Spokesman in 2004. This little volume has circulated widely, particularly in Japan.*

These poems all have their roots in one late afternoon at the 'War Ag' land workers' hostel outside Ponteland, Northumberland. The gang of workers had just returned from another sweltering day of 'labour on the land' – draining and ditching. As we entered the hostel we got the news that the first American Atom Bomb had been dropped on Japan, on the city of Hiroshima. It was the first time we had heard of that place that was to become a universal symbol of man's inhumanity towards his fellow-men.

We had become accustomed to air raids and 'buzz-bombs' and to our own casualty lists at home and abroad. But this new weapon left us nonplussed and incredulous. The date was August 6th, 1945. Its world-wide significance was at that time beyond our comprehension, and we did not realise that the date was to become an international anniversary for peace.

Three days later, on August 9th, we received the news of an even larger and more powerful plutonium bomb that had been dropped on the city of Nagasaki and had almost completely devastated it. The name was known to me only as the home of Madame Butterfly. But we began to realise the enormity of these acts of war that had annihilated hundreds of thousands of civilians.

At that time, all I knew about Japan was from my wartime readings of Arthur Waley's translation of *The Tale of Genji*. When peace was declared, I was liberated and started reading English or French or German translations of Japanese literature, ancient and modern. I also studied the history of Japanese art.

It was this passion for oriental painting

that led me to visit, in London, the first exhibition of paintings devoted to the themes of atomic bomb horrors. They were by Iri Maruki and Toshiko Akamatsu, and were shown in Europe for the first time in 1955. These vividly realistic paintings made such a profound impression upon me that I went straight back to my room and wrote in longhand, at a single draft, the poem, 'Ghosts, Fire, Water' which I took straight back to the gallery, and laid it in the book of visitors' comments (see below). Then I returned home and typed it out without any alterations and sent it to Kingsley Martin at *The New Statesman,* which had already published some of my work. It was rejected, without comment.

By that time, I had received a response from the woman who had organised the exhibition, expressing her admiration and gratitude, and urging me to send it to British newspapers and periodicals. I sent out many copies but they were all either ignored or politely rejected. However, I managed to include it in my next volume of poems, *The Descent into the Cave* (Oxford University Press), two years later, in 1957. There were no reviews mentioning the poem.

In 1959, I took up my first post in Japan, teaching English literature in Tohoku University in Sendai. As I later described in my volume of autobiography, *I, of All People* (Weidenfeld and Nicolson, 1988), the British Council did everything they could to prevent my appointment and departure, after interrogating me in their London offices.

In Japan, I visited Hiroshima and Nagasaki as soon as possible, and wrote my impressions of Hiroshima in 1960, 'No More Hiroshimas', which appeared in my new collection, *Refusal to Conform* (OUP, 1963). On various other visits to those cities I wrote 'The Lantern-Floating Festival', 'White Shadows', 'Hiroshima Revisited (1982)', 'Friends of the Neutron Bomb', 'The Carol of the Four Wise Men', 'Our New Baby' and various other poems that were widely published and commented on in Japan – but not in Britain.

I collected my A-Bomb poems in a volume entitled *No More Hiroshimas* in 1983 and sent it to all the British publishers who still published poetry. It was rejected by all of them. So I decided to publish it myself, at my own expense, and as I was then in the early 1980s teaching in Kyoto, I called my press 'Kyoto Editions'. I had discovered, in the enormous Kinokuniya bookstore in Osaka's Umeda Station, a department that renewed and bound student theses, pamphlets and poetry collections. I designed the cover, with my name translated into Japanese by Makoto Tamaki.

When the book was ready, I sent out copies to all the British press, where it was ignored. No magazine mentioned it. So I just kept sending out copies to friends and anyone I thought might be interested in it, until the first printing was exhausted. I had it reprinted by the bookshop, and by 1984 it had gone through four editions. I stamped the Peace Symbol in red on each cover.

Twenty years later, I was inspired to send a copy to Professor Ken Coates at the Bertrand Russell Peace Foundation. He at once offered to print it as a real book. So here it is, at long last.

*   *   *

Ghosts, fire, water

On the Hiroshima panels by Iri Maruki and Toshiko Akamatsu

These are the ghosts of the unwilling dead,
Grey ghosts of that imprinted flash of memory
Whose flaming and eternal instant haunts
The speechless dark with dread and anger.

Grey, out of pale nothingness their agony appears.
Like ash they are blown and blasted on the wind's
Vermilion breathlessness, like shapeless smoke
Their shapes are torn across the paper sky.

These scarred and ashen ghosts are quick
With pain's unutterable speech, their flame-cracked flesh
Writhes and is heavy as the worms, the bitter dirt;
Lonely as in death they bleed, naked as in birth.

They greet each other in a ghastly paradise,
These ghosts who cannot come with gifts and flowers.
Here they receive each other with disaster's common love,
Covering one another's pain with shrivelled hands.

They are not beautiful, yet beauty is in their truth.
There is no easy music in their silent screams,
No ordered dancing in their grief's distracted limbs.
Their shame is ours. We, too, are haunted by their fate.

In the shock of flame, their tears brand our flesh,
We twist in their furnace, and our scorching throats
Parch for the waters where the cool dead float.
We press our lips upon the river where they drink, and drown.

Their voices call to us, in pain and indignation:
'This is what you have done to us!'
Their accusation is our final hope. Be comforted.
Yes, we have heard you, ghosts of our indifference,

We hear your cry, we understand your warnings.
We, too, shall refuse to accept our fate!
Haunt us with the truth of our betrayal
Until the earth's united voices shout refusal, sing your peace!

Forgive us, that we had to see your passion to remember
What we must never again deny: *Love one another.*

London, 1955

No More Hiroshimas by James Kirkup is available from
www.spokesmanbooks.com, price £6.99

The Titanic and The Herald

George Lansbury

George Lansbury's book The Miracle of Fleet Street: The Story of the Daily Herald *has just reappeared after being out of print for many years (price £15 from www.spokesmanbooks.com). This short excerpt records how the* Herald *broke the news about what really happened when the* Titanic *went down.*

The Daily Herald's *report of the Leeds Convention of June 1917, entitled* British Labour and the Russian Revolution, *is also available from Spokesman, price £3.95.*

As the first issue of the *Daily Herald* went to press on April 15, 1912, the *Titanic* was sinking. The ship had been pronounced unsinkable. On this first voyage it was trying to make a speed record with the Chairman of the White Star Line, Bruce Ismay, on board. At first faked messages of 'all's well' were sent out, but it was soon realized that 1,300 persons were drowned. As soon as it realized this, the *Daily Herald* struck a distinctive note. W. R. Titterton was sent to Southampton to meet the rescued seamen and passengers. On April 18 the following appeared:

> 'Mr Bruce Ismay, Chairman of the White Star Line, has been saved … Why is it that so few of the steerage passengers have been saved?'

It was not till the 26th that the full story was known, and then, under the 'streamer': 'Women and Children Last!' the *Daily Herald* published a biting analysis. It pointed out the 121 steerage women and children were saved, 134 were drowned; 246 first and second class women and children were saved, and only twenty drowned; fifty-eight of the 173 first-class men passengers were saved. More than half the steerage children were drowned. The following biting words were printed:

> 'Where were those fifty-three steerage children, Mr Ismay, when you saved yourself?' The White Star Line's profits were pilloried as follows: 'They have paid 30 per cent to their shareholders and they have sacrificed 51 per cent of the steerage children. They have gone to sea criminally under-equipped with means of life-saving; they have neglected boat drill; they have filled their boat with cooks and valets, with pleasure gardens and luxurious lounges; they have done all this to get big profits and please the first-class passengers.

And when the catastrophe came they hastened to get their first-class passengers and their Chairman safely away. Fifty-three children remained to die. They were steerage passengers! One hundred and thirty-four women and children were slain. They were steerage passengers!'

Anticipating what was to come, the *Daily Herald* denounced firstly the Board of Trade for its criminal negligence, and the appointment of Lord Mersey (previously named Bigham) to head the British Inquiry, which was delayed and dragged out interminably. It recalled Lord Mersey's behaviour in the Penruddock case:

'That was a case of infamous cruelty to a child. The cruelty was undoubted, the infamy glaring. The sentence was nominal. The defendant was a woman of good station. *A first-class passenger...* Here is a case of steerage children dead and a rich company on its defence. What is likely to be Lord Mersey's judgment here?'

Jack Jones

'Ten commandments were taught in the socialist Sunday schools, but not those one heard in church. I remember particularly:

Honour good men and women, be courteous to all, bow down to none.

Do not hate or speak evil of anyone; do not be revengeful, but stand up for your rights and resist oppression.

Do not be cowardly. Be a friend to the weak and love justice.

Remember that the good things of the earth are produced by labour. Whoever enjoys them without working for them is stealing the bread of the workers.

Observe and think in order to discover the truth. Do not believe what is contrary to reason, and never deceive yourself or others.

Do not think that they who love their own country must hate and despise other nations, or wish for war, which is a remnant of barbarism.

Look forward to the day when all men and women will be free citizens of one community and live together as equals in peace and righteousness.'

From *Union Man*, Jack Jones' Autobiography

Jack Jones told us he had respected those ideas throughout his life and tried to be guided by them.

Not only millions of trade union members, but millions of pensioners and the poor of the whole country have every reason to be grateful to Jack Jones, who fought throughout his long life to live up to those principles.

Reviews

New Labour's Inequality

John Hills, Tom Sefton and Kitty Stewart (editors), *Towards a More Equal Society? Poverty, Inequality and Policy since 1997: Case Studies on Poverty, Place & Policy*, **Policy Press, 432 pages, paperback ISBN 9781847422019, £22.99**
Kate Pickett, Richard G. Wilkinson, *The Spirit Level: Why more equal societies almost always do better*, **Allen Lane, 320 pages, hardback. ISBN 9781846140396, £20**

The New Labour administrations of both Tony Blair and Gordon Brown have been sharply criticised in the current financial crisis for their obeisance to the City of London, their deregulation of financial activity, and reliance on a supposedly self-regulating market. Much less has been said about their original promise to create a more equal society. Now these two books have been published, which examine in close detail the actual results of government social policies in the decade after New Labour came to power with a massive majority in 1997, and held on to power with only slightly reduced majorities in the two subsequent elections. The period was one of steady economic growth and low inflation, which should have provided the opportunity to build a more equal society in Britain, following the glaring increase in inequalities during the previous Conservative administrations of Margaret Thatcher and John Major.

The evidence presented in the big book edited by Hills, Sefton and Stewart, under the auspices of the Joseph Rowntree Foundation, reveals that, in the event, some very slight reduction in the gap between the income of the top 20% of UK income earners and the bottom 20% was achieved in the first seven years of New Labour. After that, the gap opened up again, most especially between the top 1%, and 0.1%, and the rest. The UK remained the most unequal society of all the developed industrial societies with the exception of the United States and Portugal. In Tony Blair's most fervently promised undertaking, the ending of child poverty, some measures making for improvements were made, but these too failed, even before the disasters of 2008 overtook New Labour. Before these disasters, the poverty of pensioners had not been addressed and the credit crisis was threatening all pensions, while high figures of employment among men and women, which had helped to reduce poverty levels, had begun to collapse as the credit crisis unfolded.

In summarising the trends before and after 1997 in 31 different indicators of poverty and social exclusion, the results of the studies made by the eighteen authors published in the book, the editors, Hills, Sefton and Stewart, conclude that just under half the indicators, 14, were better and the rest either steady (9) or worse (8); but in relating the first five years of Government to the second, as many as half were better in the first but only one in eight in the second.

'Education, education, education' was Tony Blair's trumpet call at his Election, and there is no doubt that much money has been spent by his Government on this public service, with a large increase from 4.7% to 5.5% of the national income (GDP). This involved much higher spending per pupil and reduced class numbers, especially in disadvantaged schools and areas, along with new pre-school provision, such as Sure Start. The question being asked by the authors of the chapter on 'New Labour's top priority' is how far the stubborn relationship between social disadvantage and under achievement' is being broken. There is no word in the chapter on the continuing tax advantages of private schools, which cater for 15% of the population but supply most of the entrants to Oxford and Cambridge, and most of the judges, barristers, senior civil servants and journalists. Even within the state system the academic/vocational division remains, with 'grammar' and 'secondary modern' selection at the age of 11 continuing in many areas, and with new 'academies' receiving private, often 'faith' based, endowments. The gaps here seem likely to grow as both New Labour and Tory policies alike move towards more privatisation and 'marketisation' in schooling. In Higher Education the aim of achieving 50% of post-school men and women in universities was never reached, and the proportion particularly of adult students fell back sharply when fees were introduced in 2005. Adult education has, indeed, been the main victim of New Labour's recent cuts, made in the mistaken belief that skills training can take place without some basic education in a situation where at least a quarter of the population, even in the workplace, are not functionally literate and a third are innumerate, according to the Government's own 2006 Treasury Review by Lord Leitch.

After education, health has been the great recipient of New Labour government funding. Once again privatisation, especially of capital cost through Private Finance Initiative funding, and a belief in 'reform' with the aim of greater personal choice, have been the enemy of egalitarian aims. A service that was once intended to be universally free at the point of delivery, except for a payment for medicines, dentistry and spectacles by all but school children, pensioners and those on benefit, has come to be supplemented for many by private provision through individual insurance. The time of many doctors has become divided between their public patients and their private patients. The old hierarchy of medical superintendents, consultants, registrars, almoners, matrons, staff nurses and others has been replaced by a plethora of managers at every level, with targets set from on high for patient turnover, waiting time, delivery and cost.

A succession of studies in the book describe how several different groups have fared under New Labour, which might be expected to be disadvantaged and even excluded in an unequal society. The first and largest of these is, of course, women, whose position is described in several chapters. While girls' attainment at school now far surpasses that of boys, the gap in earnings remains the widest among all industrialised economies. The earnings gap has been narrowed under New Labour for full-time employment, but is still very wide for part-time employment, partly as a result of allowance for flexible hours. For all higher posts the glass ceiling is still firmly in place. On the other hand, New Labour's policy of encouraging women, especially single parents, to find work, and take the advantages of tax credits, has greatly reduced poverty levels. In health the picture is much less rosy. 'Inequalities have worsened among women to a significantly greater extent than among men,' is how the chapter on health concludes the evidence. 'This is true,' the authors write, 'across a wide range of indicators, from life expectancy to obesity; from mental health to cardio-vascular disease.'

Other chapters cover the way in which ethnic minorities and migrants have fared under New Labour. There is no doubt that, with few exceptions, educational levels have risen and unemployment levels have declined for ethnic minorities. Some groups have done better than others, and this is particularly true of the Indians. However, this has not eradicated ethnic inequalities. Employment inequality remains, despite little evidence that foreign competition has undermined local employment. However, the prospects after the credit crisis do not look good for ethnic minorities or immigrants, because strong prejudices remain and will become active in a period of rising unemployment. The further prejudice that ethnic minorities and immigrants make greater use of the health service than others has no foundation.

New Labour began its administration with a great sweep of programmes to reduce the wide differences in well-being between neighbourhoods in the United Kingdom. Examples were the New Deal for Communities and the Neighbourhood Renewal Fund. The research recorded in several chapters of the book suggest that there was subsequently a marked tailing off of such local initiatives in favour of more centralised solutions. Northern Ireland seems to have suffered particular neglect. Unemployment rates continued to be much higher in the north of England and in Scotland, Wales and Ireland, and the financial crisis is likely to make this worse.

Finally, the Joseph Rowntree Foundation book contains a chapter towards its end which compares UK experience of reducing inequality under New Labour with that of other industrialised countries. In the field of education, participation in education of children between 15 and 19, science and maths results and measures of health and well-being of 11 to 15 year olds have all improved enough to push the UK up the international rankings. So has the child poverty rate in non-working households. On the other hand, indicators of general child poverty, measured after taxes and transfers, and of teenage birth rates, which improved at first under New Labour, were not maintained. Worst of all, income inequality and literacy rates have worsened relatively, and continued failure of child poverty improvement would be serious. So would continuation of the inherited problem of low pay and the relatively low level of skills in the UK.

Comparison of inequality in the UK with that in other countries is the main subject of the second book under review, the so-called *Spirit Level* written by Pickett and Wilkinson, which seeks to understand 'why more equal societies almost always do better'. That is to say that not only the unequal members do better, but that the whole society's performance is better. The facts are plain: that among the developed economies the more unequal societies have less sense of well being, are more violent, suffer more mental illness, take more drugs and alcohol, are generally less healthy with a greater incidence of obesity, and that, ironically, these problems have worsened as average incomes and wealth have increased. The authors are concerned to answer the question, 'why should that be?' Their first answer points to the stresses of life and the pressures of consumerism and envy, as old communities and hierarchies give way to a universal individualism. But they pursue the question in a succession of chapters on different issues – on mental health and drug and alcohol abuse, on physical health, obesity and life expectancy, on educational performance, on teenage births and deprivation, on violence, prisons and punishment, and on social mobility – before considering the basis for a better society.

The result is a fascinating story with deep insights into the human condition. On each of these issues a comparison is made by the authors from the available evidence for each of the developed industrial countries, and also for each of the states of the US, with the degree of inequality recorded. On every issue the worst incidence correlates with the worst social inequality. The authors accept that this does not prove that inequalities are the cause of the problems. The inequalities might arise from the bad experiences, not the other way round. But the great number of cases of correlation with inequalities suggests otherwise. It might also happen that a concentration of population suffering inequalities might simply be outnumbering the rest. However, in the cases of mental illness, drug and alcohol abuse, obesity, teenage pregnancy, homicide and other violence, it is not at all necessarily among the less equal that these misfortunes occur. Rather the opposite is true.

This leaves us with two questions: why should social inequality have these unfortunate effects, and why are they getting worse? It cannot be said that all these misfortunes are just part of the human condition, because in societies, both in different countries and in the different US states, where there is less inequality, things are much better. The authors do suggest that in early human evolution we have a dual ape inheritance – one more competitive like the chimpanzees, one more co-operative like the bonobos. *Homo sapiens* perhaps survived through a combination of both, capable of adapting to different circumstances. What has happened in developed economies today is that competition has been encouraged at the expense of co-operation, with very stressful results. Many of our illnesses – depression, violence, over-eating, drug and alcohol abuse, early deaths – can be shown to be the result of increased stress. Societies where competition is much less, and traditions of co-operation have survived the onslaught of consumerism, have done much better.

In their last chapters the authors raise the environmental question of the survival of the planet earth, and take hope from the human capacity for co-operation and from the fact that we can live very well without all the energy-using consumer goods and services that surround us. Cuba, they give as an example of such co-operative survival, where health and education standards are high, and much assistance is given to developing countries. If those of us in the developed industrial countries could but agree to reduce massively our carbon consumption to a reasonable allowance and, on the way, pay the developing countries for their unused carbon allowance, we might all survive. It does not require a sudden revolutionary change, so the authors believe, but small step-by-step determined measures. They are being very optimistic, but they can point to the much higher contributions from Cuba and from the more equal, developed societies to aid for developing countries. Certainly there are enough resources, with the important exception of oil, still available on the planet for all to live comfortably if we could only distribute them more equally. If only?

Michael Barratt Brown

Miners

Lewis Jones, *Cwmardy and We Live*, Parthian Books and The Library of Wales, 882 pages including a foreword by Hywel Francis MP, paperback ISBN 1902638832, £9.99

Cwmardy is Lewis Jones's fictional name for a mining valley closely resembling Clydach Vale off the Rhondda Valley in South Wales. His carefully written novel describes the life and times of the Roberts family of mineworkers in the early years of the twentieth century. The story is about the struggle of coal miners to establish an effective trade union – and the equally determined methods of the mine owners to prevent such representation. Those methods included strike breaking by recruiting workers into company unions, intimidation and blacklisting of union activists, lockouts and the use of an enlarged police force and the military.

We Live is a second novel and a sequel, published posthumously two years later in 1939, continuing the story of the principal characters, Len Roberts and his wife Mary, both Communist Party activists, until Len's death in Spain as a member of the International Brigade resisting the Fascist revolution. Apart from this latter detail, which perhaps was written by a survivor of Lewis Jones, the novels can be seen as largely autobiographical. Lewis Jones was himself a coal miner from the age of 12, a checkweighman, later a student at the London Central Labour College, a Communist Party activist, and a Glamorgan county councillor.

The novels provide much authentic detail of the domestic and working lives of miners and their families. At work there was only weak regulation of such matters as adequate ventilation and adequate supplies of roof supports. Electric cap lamps came much later, and working lights were flame safety lamps whose light output was less than the candles used in non-gassy mines. Nystagmus, a vision defect associated with work in such conditions, became a recognised industrial disease. Dust diseases caused the deaths of more than 500 miners a year in the United Kingdom until the 1970s. Fatal injuries from falls of ground, the use of vehicles and machinery, fires, explosions and inundations and other causes exceeded 1,000 a year at the start of the century. In the fifty years between 1903 and 1952, 50,502 miners were killed in the UK. In 1987-8 the total number of miners killed in the nationalised British Coal mines was eight.

At work there were infestations of rodents and insects, and negligible provision for personal hygiene. Pit head baths were not generally provided until the 1930s. Miners' wives and daughters were the unpaid workers of the industry because laundered work clothes were not provided until long after nationalisation. The use of a galvanised steel bath in front of the kitchen fire was a daily routine, even when the mineworker had presented himself for work below ground and returned home because he was not offered work that day.

The author's dramatic accounts of lockouts, riots, picketing and a 'stay-down' strike are recognisably based on real events, with understatement rather than hyperbole. The miners of the Rhondda Valley have been described by historians as the most militant in Wales.[1] Their objectives from the previous century had included public ownership of the industry,[2] and the novels provide plenty of fact-based explanations for that. They also attribute the Cwmardy miners' frustration with their union full-time agent's friendly relationship with the mine owners as a cause of much militancy. The agent, called Ezra, is Mary's father, who supported Len as a young union activist. There are similarities between Ezra and William Abraham, known as Mabon, born in 1842, who became a Rhondda miners' agent and later the Lib-Lab MP for the Rhondda. Ezra in retirement from the union became an office employee of the mine owner, a fictional Lord Cwmardy, who later walked eight miles at the head of Ezra's funeral procession to a crematorium.

In the real events in the Rhondda, company recruited strike-breakers were protected by extra police drafted from distant forces. Pickets and protesters were assaulted in baton charges, arrested, prosecuted and imprisoned. The author of *Cwmardy* has 'Big Jim' Roberts, the hard drinking Boer war veteran father of Len, felling a policeman for manhandling his wife. In other confrontations the author comfortably left out much detail of real events. Miners resisted baton charges with pickaxe handles – colliers' mandrills with the steel removed. Using a mandrill to cut coal for several hours a shift is a skill not found in many policemen.[3] Miners also knew all about horses, and could bring down a mounted policeman without serious injury to the horse using nothing more than a pointed broom handle.

The police were supported by the military in South Wales in 1895, 1898 and 1910, on the initiatives of magistrates or Chief Constables often in response to calls from mine owners. Some magistrates were mine owners. In November 1910, Winston Churchill as Home Secretary appointed Major-General Nevil Macready to be in charge of troops and other forces. Home Office correspondence and Hansard records of debates in the House of Commons, quoted by R Page Arnot[4], show that the intention of the Home Office had been to disabuse the mine owners of the notion that such deployments were at their discretion, to assign costs to the local authority, and to assert the authority of central government. On November 8th, Churchill delayed the deployment of troops from Swindon and ordered that cavalry remain at Cardiff. On 19th November 1910, he replied by telegram to a letter from the Chief Constable of Glamorgan:

'Your letter of the 18th; you are quite right to act vigorously with your police force against serious riot. A certain amount of minor friction is, however, inseparable from the present situation. Both sides are unreasonable in many ways, and I should recommend you to go gently in small matters. – Churchill.'

Michael Thomas in *The Death of an Industry*[5] probably used local newspaper accounts to record that, on November 26 1910, at Ely colliery near Tonypandy, Captain Paterson in command of a squad of the Somerset Light Infantry with fixed bayonets and live ammunition helped to restore order after an attack on police who were protecting would-be strike breakers. No ammunition was used, but one of General Macready's reports contains mention of 'a little gentle persuasion with the bayonet' in Tonypandy on November 21st. His same report states that no casualties were reported, but that

'Many young men of the valley found that sitting down was accompanied with a certain amount of discomfort for several days.'[6]

One of the accounts of a stay-down strike, which one hopes is fictional, is of the potentially murderous use of a 30 hundredweight coal tram filled with horse dung made to run away down an inclined underground roadway by the striking miners, whose lamps were no longer alight, to disperse officials and others who were approaching to remove them from the mine.

Representation by an effective trade union was essential to resolve such conflict. The coal trade was volatile, especially in South Wales with its high rank, low volatile coals favoured by the merchant navy and the Royal Navy. In good times miners' earnings were twice those of agricultural workers, and the profits from the colliery owners' investments were vast. Many of the growing immigrant population of the valleys had houses with cold water taps and water closets, rare in rural areas. Miners investing their labour and their lives needed a minimum wage to maintain their ability for physical work, and to mitigate casual employment on varying piece-work price lists, and arbitrary conditions such as payment only for lump coal.

The novels have relevance today not least because our capitalist system once more requires urgent regulation to protect people and the planet. The UK Labour government has cause to re-examine its New Labour claims that it is no longer necessary to have in public ownership some of the means of production, distribution and exchange. The management of the credit crisis and its effects is proving difficult, and one suspects that the public are ready to be persuaded that having the banks in public ownership, rather than just absorbing £200 billions of public money, may be a good idea after all. Readers of the novels will find some vindication of the Marxist analyses of people such as Lewis Jones who saw human rights abuses, links between industry and the military, Fascism and war as endemic characteristics of capitalism. If he were alive today he would surely wonder why the world spends more than one trillion dollars a year on weapons, while no such sum is yet made available to mitigate climate change, resource depletion, pollution, hunger and disease.

A preface to the novel *Cwmardy* states that Lewis Jones joined the Communist Party in the 1920s, but an interesting foreword by Hywel Francis, the son of Dai Francis, a Spanish civil war veteran, includes an account by Billy Griffiths, another Spanish war veteran, which suggests that Lewis Jones was no Stalinist. At the Seventh World Congress of the Communist International in Moscow, in 1935, thousands rose from their seats when Stalin arrived but Lewis Jones failed to stand. He embarrassed the British delegation and was reprimanded by the party on his return to Britain. Hywel Francis is the author of *Miners Against Fascism* (1984) and is now Labour MP for Aberavon.[7] His foreword makes clear his enthusiasm for the re-publication of these novels by Parthian and The Library of Wales – a Welsh Assembly Government project to make Welsh literature written in English more widely available.

Christopher Gifford

References

1. For example Professor V C Allen in *The Militancy of British Miners,* The Moor Press, Shipley, 1981
2. *Democracy in the Mines – Some documents of the Controversy on Mines Nationalisation up to the Time of the Sankey Commission,* Selected and edited by Ken Coates, Spokesman Books, 1974
3. *South Wales Miners – a History of the South Wales Miners' Federation 1898-1914,* p194, Robin Page Arnot, George Allen and Unwin, 1967
4. Ibid
5. Michael Thomas in *The Death of an Industry,* Colben Systems Pte Ltd, 2004, p49.
6. Robin Page Arnot; op. cit.
7. Also co-author with David Smith of *The Fed – a History of the South Wales Miners in the Twentieth Century,* Lawrence and Wishart Ltd, 1980.

Red October

Margarita Tupitsyn (Editor), *Rodchenko & Popova: Defining Constructivism*, Tate Publishing, 192 pages, paperback ISBN 9781854377968, £24.99

Tumultuous years followed the Russian Revolution of October 1917. While the war in France raged on, civil war engulfed large tracts of Russia as the White armies, supported by Churchill among others, sought to overthrow the new Bolshevik regime.

Russia's cities starved as grain supplies from the countryside dried up. Millions of poorer peasants produced barely enough to subsist. More prosperous ones, known as kulaks, tended to horde any surplus as the currency collapsed and everyday goods became unavailable. Requisitioning, as part of 'war communism', forcibly extracted some limited supplies for the newly created Red Army, which was fighting the Whites with notable success. But millions of people left the cities in search of food in the countryside. The situation was made much worse when drought caused the harvest to fail, which gave rise to a terrible famine that spread throughout the Volga basin and beyond, starting in spring 1921, and continuing into the following year.

At the landmark Tenth Congress of the Russian Communist Party (Bolsheviks), in March 1921, while Red Army soldiers fought to suppress a rebellion by sailors based at the fortress of Kronstadt, Lenin argued for a New Economic Policy, or NEP. The survival of the new Soviet state was in question, as Kronstadt and other rebellions indicated. The sailors were demanding concessions for workers and peasants, as well as the free election of Soviets. Lenin struggled to address some of these grievances. Under the New Economic Policy, limited private trade was to be permitted. This was particularly directed at restoring agricultural production in the countryside so that, in turn, the cities and their industrial workers could be fed. Kulaks could once again employ other peasants in order to boost production. Lenin envisaged that this policy might continue for a number of years. It survived his death, in 1924, when Bukharin became its leading advocate, but was eventually abandoned by Stalin, in 1928, notwithstanding his earlier support for the policy, in opposition to Trotsky's criticisms.

So it comes as a refreshing surprise that, during all this tumult, the artists Aleksandr Rodchenko and Liubov Popova, together with members of their circle such as the poet Vladimir Mayakovsky , were engaged, often humorously and always creatively, in their own representational constructions of the new Soviet state. Geometry, pattern and line (frequently straight) preoccupied them, whilst colour was ultimately distilled to 'Pure Red Colour, Pure Yellow Colour, Pure Blue Colour' in Rodchenko's three oil-on-canvas panels of 1921. Typography was usually red and black, strikingly bold, and geometrically varied. Its influence endures to this day.

For these artists were embarked on the new Soviet adventure. There was a studied consciousness of equality. 'The Female Journalist', in Kuleshov's 1927 film of that title, (for which Rodchenko designed sets), is confronted by a woman cleaner sweeping papers from the newsroom floor. They meet on a wooden gangway, the journalist in her modern dress and bob haircut, the cleaner anonymous under a broad-brimmed hat, back to camera. Nearby, the presses roll, great reels of paper waiting their turn as printers tend the mighty machine. The heyday of NEP was already passing, and the 'nepmen' and business women increasingly satirised.

Film flourished in Russia during the years after the Revolution. Rodchenko's 1925 poster design for Sergei Eisenstein's 'Battleship Potemkin', a landmark in Soviet film, includes a notably conventional drawing of the infant in its runaway pram descending an imaginary stairway. Rodchenko's interest in the camera was growing, as he himself recorded in a beautiful 'Self-Caricature', executed in gouache and pencil, also in 1925.

Popova was already dead. She and her young son were carried off by scarlet fever during the epidemic of 1924. A posthumous exhibition of her work was put on in Moscow, for which Rodchenko designed a catalogue with characteristically monumental typography on the cover, reflecting aspects of Popova's own typographical style.

She had evidently been much engaged in designing fabric and clothing prior to her death. One delicate design in gouache has the hammer in blue and the sickle coloured red. (The Tate Modern has produced aprons and kerchiefs made from the fabric for sale in its shop.) But her dress designs, such as those for summer 1924, usually feature more abstract designs. As private trade grew under the New Economic Policy, Rodchenko and Popova designed simple advertisements to promote the products of the Red October biscuit factory and other state enterprises.

That such endeavours were termed 'Constructivism' was what the recent exhibition at the Tate Modern set about trying to define. In doing so, it mounted an exhibition that is full of creativity, enthusiasm and experimentation. The young Soviet Union, as represented here, was light years away from its feudal, tsarist antecedent. It looked forward to the coming century, not back, and anticipated much of the design and taste that came to characterise modernity in the decades that were to follow. That influence is far from spent, as this exhibition made crystal clear.

In 1925, Rodchenko accompanied his design for the Workers' Club, replete with reading room, chess-boards, and films, to the Paris Exhibition, where it was a great success. The young Soviet Union was emerging, by degree, from international isolation. The recent Tate Modern exhibition, and its excellent catalogue, emphasise how high their hopes were.

Tony Simpson

Doubt Everything

Jan Willem Stutje, *Ernest Mandel: A Rebel's Dream Deferred*, Verso, 392 pages, hardback ISBN 9781844673162, £19.99

Ernest Mandel was a remarkable man, and I suppose he has to be described as a charismatic orator. In general, I rather prefer my politics without charisma, which is commonly used to bedazzle and befuddle the innocent punters. But Mandel was truly exceptional.

I first met him when I was invited to visit the 5th World Congress of the Fourth International in 1957. He delivered a report, which was over two hours long, speaking in voluble French. He then delivered it again in German, and finally he gave it to us in English. I don't really remember much of what he said, and I don't really approve of very long speeches, leave alone long speeches in three languages. But I am bound to admit that this was a *tour de force*, even if I have not remembered it. Mandel was a most impressive person, personally a charmer, and intellectually formidable.

None the less, the 5th World Congress of the Fourth International was a nearly total shambles, and I found it distinctly off-putting. There was one notable public quarrel, which I could understand, and one more concealed dispute at which I could only guess. The public rumpus was between the majority of the South American delegation, which was quite numerous, and the majority of the Europeans. The South Americans were led by Juan Posadas, who was also good at long speeches, although the long speeches were not so good in content. Posadas believed that the third World War was inevitable, and he devoutly wished that the Russians and Chinese would get on with it. Many of the Trotskyists could be faulted in their attitude to this analysis, but Posadas had major faults.

I was already a disciple of Bertrand Russell, and a passionately convinced proponent of nuclear disarmament. In particular, I believed that any future World War would very likely mean the end of the species, and I therefore thought that everyone should bend their efforts to preventing it rather than encouraging any of the belligerents. This meant that I had no sympathy whatever with Posadas, whatever might be his opinions on lesser questions, and I was underwhelmed by this Congress, even though I met some extraordinarily interesting people there. There was the Norwegian Socialist MP who had given asylum to Trotsky in exile, for instance, and there was young Lily Peng, the daughter of the venerable Chinese leader. I spent some pleasant hours on the beach with her, while the comrades were dutifully sharpening their applied dogmatics, in closed sessions to which visitors were not invited.

It was easy to see Mandel as a different kettle of fish from the head bangers. Subsequent generations have frequently wondered how such a very clever man could be so comprehensively involved in the affairs of the Fourth International, which has generated continuous factional squabbles and sectarian disputes on a truly inhibiting scale. Mandel himself was a polemicist to match the best of them. But he could also be an inspiring teacher, and indeed he inspired a remarkable following among European students. I was one of those who fell under his spell, and I have never regretted the fact, because he taught me a great deal. But perhaps the most important thing he taught me was to stand on my own feet, and not to follow anyone, be they never so persuasive.

Mandel was a loyal partisan of Trotsky and wrote what is possibly the best book on Trotsky's ideas. (*Trotsky – a Study in the Dynamic of his Thought*, Verso, 1979.)

Jan Willem Stutje has given us a large-scale biography, and it will certainly help to keep Mandel's memory fresh. It explains his induction into political activism during the Second World War. He grew up in Belgium, and was thrust into political activism during the Nazi occupation. Ernest's father was a Polish socialist, highly skilled in the diamond trade, who had, during the First World War, fled to Belgium and then Holland in order to avoid conscription into the Austrian army. Ernest was ten years old when Hitler came to absolute power, so that, in his late teens, when the Nazis overran most of Western Europe, he was ready to join the resistance.

He had joined a small Trotskyist group in Antwerp in 1939, and at the age of sixteen he was arrested for leafleting the German soldiers of the occupation army. He was released from internment camp with the complicity of the German guards with whom he argued, who had themselves been members of the forbidden Social Democratic and Communist Parties in Germany in pre-Hitler days before their suppression. This experience confirmed him in an internationalist outlook, which refused to condemn whole nations for the actions of those set in authority over them.

Jan Willem Stutje describes Mandel's activities in the resistance, which became more and more audacious as the war wore on.

But these activities did not result in the overthrow of capitalism, as the Fourth International had ardently hoped. Neither did it bring an end to the rule of bureaucracy in Russia. Instead, Russian-sponsored governments were put in place all across Eastern Europe, and the influence of Stalinism became even more pervasive. This influence brought the most intelligent governors of capitalism into a much more realistic assessment of their situation. The German and French élites clearly decided that readying themselves for the third World War might be a mistake, and under Monnet's inspiration, they established the European Coal and Steel Community, as a prototype for a European federalism which would, by fusing the coal and steel industries, both eliminate the possibility of further intra-European wars, and, as significantly, help generate possibilities for a regime of European welfare which might stand some hope of stemming the advance of Communist Parties, already the largest in Italy and France. Trotskyists took a long time to catch up with these events, even when they were very clever, but it is not surprising that they provoked strenuous ideological debates.

By the time that things had settled down in the 1950s, most Trotskyists had decided that they should devote their efforts to attempting to work within pre-established big parties of Labour. In Social Democratic Parties this was really nothing new, but in Communist Parties it involved a pretty substantial trauma, because these were still very much official formations, following the Russian line in every detail.

Mandel applied himself to his work within the Belgian Socialist Party with considerable effect. Under his influence the lively weekly, *La Gauche*, was established, followed by a Flemish sister paper. Mandel became an economic advisor to the Belgian Trade Unions, and an influential leader of the Belgian Left.

Stutje is disappointingly brief in his treatment of this episode in the Mandel story, because the campaign for 'structural reforms' and for workers' control had a resonance which exerted influence far beyond Belgium itself. I remember publishing a translation of the workers' control programme of the FGTB (socialist) trade union, and suggesting that European workers now needed to follow the classical advice of Rosa Luxembourg, and 'learn to speak Belgian'. But the leaders of the Belgian socialists themselves were not keen on speaking Belgian, and *La Gauche* was told to shut up shop. When it refused, Mandel and his closest sympathisers found themselves once more in isolation, even if they had won widespread respect.

Stutje has not quite got the story of Mandel's second visit to Cuba in focus. I secured this invitation for him when I met Fidel Castro earlier that year. I was representing the Russell Foundation in some talks we had about the developing worldwide opposition to the American war in Vietnam. Ernest subsequently made the trip to Havana with his new wife, Gisela Scholtz, a very beautiful young woman, dynamic and clever who carried a tragic burden of illness.

I assume that Castro was in no way willing to compromise his diplomatic achievements by entering into serious talks with a prominent Trotskyist leader. In this respect he differed from Che Guevara. Ernest was shown the sights, and one of the functionaries who entertained him, told me during the OLAS conference which took place shortly after his visit that, 'Your professor was not a very practical chap, but his woman was most promising, a crack shot'. I don't know what passed between my professor and his Cuban interlocutors, but the Russian invasion of Czechoslovakia in 1968 was soon to bring about an estrangement between the Cuban leadership and a wide cross-section of the European left.

It is at this point that Stutje can follow his own enthusiasms in tracing Mandel's story, by treating on his major writings on *Marxist Economic Theory*. At the time I tried very hard to find a publisher for an English translation which was finally taken up by the Merlin Press, thanks very much to the intervention of Ralph Miliband. Brian Pearce produced a splendidly readable version. The book was to appear in many other languages, and to exert an influence which helped to transform views of Marx and Marxism throughout the Western world.

Mandel had been a close correspondent and admirer of Roman Rosdolsky, the exiled Ukrainian scholar, who had acquired one of the very few copies of Marx's crucially important *Grundrisse* that existed in the West. At the time this was unknown to the overwhelming majority of Marxian specialists, although it was the real foundation upon which the later *Capital* was to rest.

Rosdolsky saw it as his special mission to analyse the *Grundrisse* and make it available to a much wider audience, because it would dispel a large number of incorrect assumptions about the 'Marxism' of Marx. His book, *The Making of Marx's Capital,* had a significant influence on Mandel, and Stutje offers a tantalising glimpse of the correspondence between the two men. Rosdolsky had a profound admiration for Trotsky but a less than reverent view of the Fourth International. In this, he shared the opinions of

Isaac Deutscher, among others. In fact, it does seem to be true that Trotsky's major influence in modern times has been exerted through the agency of people who were very far from true believers. Obviously Mandel was a true believer if ever there was one, but his mind was so open and wide ranging that he could genuinely appreciate the creative spark of Rosdolsky's thought, engaging with him as an equal.

A not totally dissimilar story could be told about Mandel's long and affectionate relationship with Ernst Bloch, another Titan whose exchanges with Mandel are rather tantalisingly glimpsed in Stutje's pages.

There is, of course, another key figure in the Mandel story, who was a core influence on his circle. This was the Greek, Michel Raptis, otherwise known as Pablo. Mandel met him when he was thirty-three years old, and thus a venerable senior among all these youthful activists. His was a significant influence, because he was devoid of the constricting sectarianism which so deformed the vision of so many of his and Mandel's co-thinkers. He led his small band of followers, in spite of their isolation and inexperience, into a heroic international effort to help the Algerian revolution to succeed. This meant that he was able to begin to implement his scheme of self-management in industry as a member of the Algerian revolutionary administration. Mandel and Pablo later quarrelled mightily, and pioneered yet another ferocious split among the kaleidoscopic schisms of the Fourth International. But Mandel had learnt much of his political style from Pablo, and the two men were reconciled towards the end of their lives. Had this happened earlier, who knows, they might both have been more effective. In a team Pablo was a powerfully practical man, and Ernest Mandel was becoming a distinguished theoretician: together, they might have achieved something solid. As a feud, they were fireworks.

Marxist Economic Theory was followed by *Late Capitalism, The Second Slump,* and *Long Waves of Capitalist Development*, together with a host of political writings and polemical tracts. The scholarly effort involved in this prodigious output was truly impressive. But it was accompanied by a level of political activism and agitation which is quite mind-boggling. Stutje shows that much of this was of dubious effect, and although I am not qualified to judge many of these matters, it does appear that there were a number of sad miscalculations. The effort to organise the Trotskyist opposition in Poland, for instance, does not appear to have been a glorious chapter in Mandel's story. If Stutje is right about it, it was a calamitous series of mistakes, if not worse.

Of course, the Polish episode was no doubt helped forward and greatly aggravated by the attention of various spooks. It does seem to me that the

Fourth International was blessed by an extraordinary fascination for spooks of all kinds. Its formative years saw an OGPU (or KGB) agent discharging its secretarial functions after the very suspicious death of Trotsky's son, Leon Sedov. Wherever different national groupings emerged thereafter their fascination for spooks seems to have been seriously disproportionate to any real impact they might have had on the political life of the countries in question.

At one time I used to think that the fissiparous nature of Trotskyism ('create two, three, many Fourth Internationals') might have been helped along by some of these agencies. But in the light of subsequent experience in the post-Trotskyist left, I am not entirely sure that the comrades needed help from these agencies when it came to inventing bizarre reasons for forming and reforming a bewildering variety of schisms.

I was involved in the movement for European Nuclear Disarmament at the same time, and I became rather impatient with some of the results of the other, less doctrinaire but equally ill-fated attempts to create a disarmament movement in Poland and elsewhere in Eastern Europe. If the road to hell is paved with good intentions, it is not necessarily true that good intentions will lead to hell. They are more likely to get stuck in the mud of reality, where greater and greater efforts of belief are required to overcome healthy agnosticism.

Rational intentions will encourage freethinking. Not for nothing, Marx told us to doubt everything. The good society will thrive on doubt, and a society that doesn't won't be good.

Ken Coates

Lucky Ashdown

Paddy Ashdown, *A Fortunate Life*, Aurum Press Ltd, 416 pages, hardback ISBN 9781845134198, £20

Slobodan Milosevic told Paddy Ashdown he was the first person to admit that the Kosovo Liberation Army (KLA) was a terrorist organisation. 'You are the first person sitting in that chair who said during these proceedings that he does not deny that the KLA was a terrorist organisation,' said Milosevic. 'Everybody before you denied that.' (source: Trial Transcript p.2402).

It was 15 March 2002, and the trial of the third President of the Federal Republic of Yugoslavia before the International Criminal Tribunal for the Former Yugoslavia in The Hague staggered on. Judge Richard May had to urge the suggestible Baron Ashdown to keep his answers brief and to the point, perhaps for fear that he might let slip other howlers. Milosevic had made a statistical presentation highlighting the spike in KLA attacks, on Albanian as well as Serb communities in Kosovo, during 1998, executed with the particular assistance of the German foreign intelligence organisation, the BND, he said.

Not that you would glean any of this from Paddy Ashdown's remarkably uninformative autobiography. According to the noble Lord, who was a witness for the prosecution, he

> ' ... tried to keep him [Milosevic] tightly confined to the events I had seen and not let him wander off into generalised diatribes about western politicians and the west's "illegal" actions in the recent war.' (p.339)

No wonder the weary Judge wasn't best pleased with the witness.

Lord Ashdown was first 'parachuted' into what had, until very recently, been the Socialist Federal Republic of Yugoslavia, in August 1992. He arrived in Sarajevo, Bosnia's capital, which was already descending into war as President Alija Izetbegovic sought to secede from the Federal Republic. Izetbegovic, who was to become Ashdown's 'friend', wanted to follow Slovenia and Croatia out of the Federation. (What did Ashdown know of Izetbegovic's other friend, Osama bin Laden, who was welcomed by Izetbegovic together with thousands of other fighters who were dispatched from Pakistan to Bosnia following the defeat and withdrawal of the Russians in Afghanistan in 1988?) These secessions from the Yugoslav Federation were being accomplished with considerable help from the Germans and, in the case of Croatia, the Americans, among others. Who sent Ashdown into Yugoslavia, at this critical juncture in its dissolution, and for what purpose, is not at all clear. But, once he was there, his appetite to interfere was given ample rein.

Not that he hadn't been warned. Fitzroy MacLean, who knew Yugoslavia well and had helped Tito's partisans liberate their country from the Nazi occupation, cautioned Ashdown against encouraging western intervention in Bosnia. He knew what he was talking about, but Ashdown wasn't listening. In fact, he didn't even know at the time that it was MacLean who was offering this advice. Ashdown had been to Yugoslavia twice in a matter of weeks, and he 'knew exactly what should happen – we should intervene'.

Who was the 'we' Ashdown had in mind? By 1995, John Major and Douglas Hurd were already seeking to withdraw British troops who had been deployed to 'safe havens' in Bosnia, which had been set up under UN auspices primarily to protect Bosniak Muslims from attacks by the Bosnian Serbs led by General Mladic. Tony Blair replaced Major in 1997, and Ashdown had a new friend at court.

It was about this time that the fuse was lit for what became NATO's ten-week-long bombardment of Yugoslavia, as it still was, in 1999. NATO pilots flew more than 38,000 missions, hitting roads, bridges, trains and not a few horse-drawn carts carrying terrified peasants, as well as urban targets including Belgrade, Novi Sad and Pristina, the largest city in Kosovo, which was then still part of the Federal Republic of Yugoslavia. Hundreds of people were killed, with many more injured. There was also widespread contamination due to the heavy use of depleted uranium weapons, about which NATO was extremely reluctant to provide information to the agencies charged with conducting a clean-up.

Ashdown doesn't play down his role in encouraging a land war in Yugoslavia. After the initial air raids on Belgrade, he had again 'set off' for the region, and was quick to encourage the use of land forces. He writes:

> 'On the day after I got back [from seeing General Mike Jackson in Macedonia], I received a call from Jonathan Powell, who was in Washington with Blair. He asked for my conclusions from the visit and I told him. He replied that Blair was about to go and see Clinton. Could I please fax my report through immediately, so that he could read it before the meeting? I did so. It was, I believe, at this meeting that Blair finally persuaded Clinton, against the counsel of his closest advisors, that he should be prepared to risk putting US troops in harm's way and start preparing for an opposed invasion if necessary.' [p.329]

It didn't come to that, thanks to the Russians, who persuaded Milosevic to withdraw his forces from Kosovo, something that NATO's increasingly desperate bombardment had failed to accomplish. Two years later, in 2001, Blair proposed Ashdown for the role of High Representative in Bosnia and Herzegovina, whose formal task it was to implement the Dayton Accords pushed through in 1995 by Bill Clinton, with Milosevic's help, as a 'Framework Agreement for Peace in Bosnia and Herzegovina'. Ashdown took up his posting in May 2002. He records his view of the job as being that he:

> 'could interfere in anything … And to help me interfere in everything if I wanted to, I had a staff … of approximately 800 and a budget of some £36 million. And to make interfering in other people's business even more fun, I had an array of formidable powers … under which I could impose laws, subject only to their eventual endorsement by the domestic parliaments, and remove officials and politicians who were blocking or undermining the implementation of the Dayton agreement.' (p.346-347)

If Ashdown interfered in the Bosnian passport granted to Osama bin Laden, or the fate of the 2,000 Mujahideen from Afghanistan who fought in the Bosnian Muslim army, (who, according to a report in *The Independent*, were subsequently expelled from the country), he doesn't see fit to tell readers of his autobiography about it. Izetbegovic's Bosnia was a key destination for Osama's cohorts once they were forced to leave Afghanistan and Pakistan, according to John Schindler, who was for many years the chief Balkan expert for the US National Security Council. (See *Spokesman 100* for Michael Barratt Brown's review of Schindler's book *Unholy Terror: Bosnia, Al Qaeda, and the Rise of Global Jihad.*) Indeed, according to Schindler, in 2002, Ashdown actually fired the one member of the Bosnian Government, Munir Alibabic, who was seriously trying to control the Mujahideen and tackle the corruption associated with their activities (Schindler p.290 onwards).

Ashdown had worked for the British secret intelligence organization known as MI6. As far as we know, that organisation seems to have a highly questionable record in Yugoslavia during its last years. It apparently swung from supporting the Serbs to a misconceived plot to assassinate President Milosevic. This plot was picked over in some detail at the long-delayed inquest into the death of Diana, Princess of Wales, in 2007-8. An MI6 witness alleged that Arkan, an irregular soldier with a fearful reputation who was born in Slovenia and grew up in Zagreb and Belgrade, was the actual target of the abortive plot. Why anyone should have thought removing Arkan from the scene might have changed the course of events in Yugoslavia was not clearly explained.

You will look in vain in Lord Ashdown's *Fortunate Life* for any real insights into US/British policy towards Yugoslavia and its destruction, or NATO's expansion eastwards towards Russia. He could have told us something interesting, and broadened our understanding, but has chosen not to do so.

Anthony Lane

Worms-Eye-View

Chris Mullin, *A View from the Foothills: The Diaries of Chris Mullin*, Profile Books, 448 pages, hardback ISBN 9781846682230, £20

In a previous incarnation we knew Chris Mullin as a sea-green incorruptible, a hammer of Labour's parliamentary right wing. Indeed, his major claim to fame as a zealous Bennite was his pamphlet which offered us a primer on how to select and de-select your Member of Parliament. In those far-off days, control of the political machine devolved on membership of the House of Commons, and all patronage depended on this. Access to Parliament was jealously restricted, and Members could not be ejected for any reason other than the gros-sest moral perfidy or severe misjudgement of the political odds. In the Bible we were told that it was easier for a camel to go through the eye of a needle than for a rich man to enter the Kingdom of Heaven. Squadrons of camels could enter and exit the Parliamentary Labour Party at will, before a loyal time-server could be evicted, be he never so incompetent or tainted with sleaze.

In this book, which reveals the modern incarnation of Chris Mullin, this pamphlet is described as a modest contribution to New Labour's resolute efforts to democratise the Labour Party. In fact, it was a shock horror contribution to the dispossession of a thoroughly disreputable section of the fortified political class, who held their Parliamentary seats as if they were a fiefdom, and were kept in place by a small retinue of officials who were empowered to squash any insurrectionary moves against them. Having survived all such squashing, the irrepressible Mullin passed over to the other side, and all the trumpets sounded. Now his *Diaries* celebrate what he calls his view from the foothills, in contradistinction to the view from the Olympian heights, where the really big sleazeballs hang out.

Mullin has given us an amusing book, in which engaging self-deprecation is the keynote. His transition to the lower ranks of the establishment followed a passionate infatuation with Tony Blair, which is one of the stranger phenomena in British Labour history. Tony Blair has been ruthlessly greedy, relentlessly reactionary, a warmonger and war criminal, and all the things that people like the young Mullin would have regarded with nausea. But as the fount of all patronage, Tony Blair became a revered object, referred to throughout this book as 'The Man', whose every gesture was regarded in awe, as a possible token of favours or chastisement to come.

The favours that were likely to come the way of Chris Mullin were not necessarily very elevatcd.

> 'Life on the lower ranks of the ministerial ladder is a vast cascade of all the things my many superiors do not wish to do. Today an invitation was passed down from Nick Raynsford's office. His private secretary's note was still attached. It read: 'This is very low priority. Suggest we pass it to Chris Mullin'. I wrote 'No' on it, and waited to see what would happen. Sure enough, within the hour, someone was in my office explaining that it was really of the highest importance ...'

Poor Chris. The higher he rose on the greasy pole, the less important the tasks he was given to perform.

An ideal spot for keeping the drudges busy and simultaneously out of mischief was, of course, on one of the desks of the Foreign Office. Chris found his perch after much nail-biting uncertainty, on the Africa desk. From time to time this mattered to his masters, when Blair was seeking to augment his votes for war in the Security Council of the United Nations. But all that diplomacy came to nothing, leaving behind itself a train of useless interviews, lunches, dinners, and (doubtless, expensive) meetings.

It was not during his ministerial incarnation that Chris Mullin shone, although no doubt he gave satisfaction. Perhaps it would have been better if he didn't.

The part of the book that is riveting describes the run up to the war in Iraq, when The Man is reported as dazzling the Parliamentary Labour Party like a Boa Constrictor. Of course, it is not the snake that harbours the secret of the hypnotism. It is the base instincts of the victims, who cannot wait to be bewitched. Chris Mullin's honest story captivates us, because he normally tries to tell things more or less as they were. But the story of Britain's descent into the Iraq war was not simply the story of a hypnotic confidence trickster, or beguiling politician. A million Iraqis died in this war, and it was obvious from the very beginning moments of shock and awe that we were living through a dreadful experience. Chris Mullin notices some of the torture. He knows quite well how bad it all was.

Surely, a time is coming when no one involved in that slaughter would be deemed fit to hold office of any kind.

Harry Jones

Engels Revived

Tristram Hunt, *The Frock-coated Communist: The Revolutionary Life of Friedrich Engels*, 464 pages, Allen Lane, hardback ISBN 9780713998528, £25

Tristram Hunt has written a worthy sequel to Francis Wheen's *Karl Marx*, but it corrects some of the under-estimation which has grown up around the contribution of the second half of the Marx-Engels collaboration. Engels tends to be depicted as the mere supplier of funds from his family's Manchester textile business to finance Marx's family during the twenty years when Marx laboured over his great work on Capital, nobly took responsibility for siring Marx's child by his house-keeper, and additionally was the editor of the last two volumes of *Capital*. It is recognised that the

Communist Manifesto was a joint work and that Engels, at an early age, wrote *The Condition of the Working Class in England* and, much later, contributed *Socialism Utopian and Scientific*, *The Origins of the Family* and *The Dialectics of Nature*. His book *Anti-Dühring* is claimed as the foundation of German socialism, but also, incorrectly, as a determinist form of scientific materialism, which led to the outrages of Stalinism.

Tristram Hunt in his book tackles all these misunderstandings and distortions. Engels' intimate knowledge of the conditions of labour exploitation in the cotton trade in the first half of the nineteenth century gave Marx the solid basis for his work on Capital. The correspondence between Engels and Marx is replete with examples of the alienation experienced by men and women workers, typical today of Chinese industrialisation, as Hunt comments. The dialectics which both Marx and Engels took from Hegel, and the revolutionary experiences they shared in 1848, cemented their friendship into an immensely productive alliance, in which the contribution of Engels, as Hunt records it, was enormous. Engels' knowledge of European languages made him naturally the corresponding secretary of the First International, co-ordinating the proletarian struggle across the continent.

One strange lacuna in Hunt's book is the slight treatment of the Paris Commune in 1871, two pages compared with a whole chapter of 30 pages devoted to 1848. This is not just a small mistake, but a big one. As a result, not only are the detailed reports missing which were made by Engels of events in France, and became the basis for Marx's *Civil War in France*, but this neglect allows Engels' support for social democracy in Germany and approval of parliamentary activity in England to appear to over-ride his absolute commitment to the inevitability and desirability of proletarian revolution.

Hunt deals with the charge that the exposition of dialectics by Engels in the *Dialectics of Nature* encouraged Stalin to justify, in the *History of the Communist Party of the Soviet Union (Bolsheviks): Short Course* and in his actions, a determinist view of Communism as an inevitable development that involved all sorts of violence. Engels, without doubt, had for his time a remarkably wide range of knowledge of scientific discoveries, including Darwin's explanation of the Origin of Species, but there is no evidence that he believed in a form of social Darwinism, which made the survival of the fittest depend upon sheer physical force. Hunt gives the charge short shrift, and adds an epilogue to the book which examines and destroys the caricature of Engels as a narrow minded, mechanistic architect of Soviet ideology. By contrast, Engels is shown in his own later writings to have held an open, critical and humane vision of scientific socialism, with support for a social democratic, parliamentary road for the proletariat, as a step towards a proletarian revolution involving violence in the last resort.

Engels' bourgeois ways are allowed for – as the 'frock-coated Communist' – his love of fox hunting (he was a member of the prestigious Cheshire Hunt), his enjoyment of good wines (the list of boxes of champagne, clarets and other wines stacked in the cellars of his Primrose Hill houses is almost endless), and his attraction to beautiful women (though his devotion to the two mill girls he married – successively Lizzy and Mary Burns – was unshakeable, and he was an early champion of women's rights). He was, perhaps, the first 'champagne socialist' – a title which my grandchildren accord to me, with rather less reason. It is this remarkable combination in Engels of pleasure in the good things of life with an unswerving commitment to socialism that so attracts me to the man, and its exposition in Tristram Hunt's book that gave me so much pleasure.

Michael Barratt Brown

Scotland Can Afford It

Alexander Moffat, Alan Riach, Linda MacDonald-Lewis, *Arts of Resistance: Poets, Portraits and Landscapes of Modern Scotland*, Luath Press, 192 pages, hardback ISBN 9781906307639, £29.99, paperback ISBN 9781906817183, £16.99

This little book follows the conversations of portrait artist Alexander Moffat, poet Alan Riach and historian Linda MacDonald-Lewis at a series of lectures given at the National Galleries of Scotland. Being two well connected artists, and possibly the close connection of their lectures with the Galleries, has allowed them to produce a volume bringing together an excellent collection of illustrations covering the period from late nineteenth century Scotland till today. Truly, it was an epoch of change socially, politically, and of technologies.

Working on the theme that the national has to be developed before engagement can be made in the international milieu, *Arts of Resistance* covers the closeness of the cultural leaders it discusses to the country's physical attributes as well as its traditions, and its adoption and development of new ideas. All this is developed during the period which

Hobsbawm called 'The Age of Extremes'. It has also been a period of improvements in transport and communications. All this started prior to the introduction of radio and television, but those media gave an impetus to the exchange of ideas. Whereas, during the age of Burns, his meetings with other artists in Edinburgh were recorded as historic events, in the period after the Second World War there were frequent meetings of our cultural élite during the Edinburgh Festival and, at other times, in Milne's Bar. Moffat's illustrations of them, individually and collectively, are included in this volume.

Having had the good fortune to work on documentary programmes recording their views and capturing them at work, it has to be remarked that those artists I met were good company. This may go a long way to explaining the encouraging and enhancing effect they have had collectively on Scottish culture.

Arts of Resistance contain many excerpts from poems by the people it discusses. But one poem they don't use perhaps encapsulates the crossover from landscape and romance to the hard political, which reveals national failings, but also the recognition of these failings, in the Scottish body politic. Hugh MacDiarmid in his *Third Hymn to Lenin* puts it thus;

> *Clever – and yet we cannot solve this problem even;*
> *Civilised – and flaunting such a monstrous sore;*
> *Christian – in flat defiance of all Christ taught;*
> *Proud of our country with this open sewer at our door,*
> *Come, let us shed all this transparent bluff,*
> *Acknowledge our impotence, the prize eunuchs of Europe,*
> *Battening on our shame, and with voices weak as bats'*
> *Proclaiming in ghoulish kirks our base immortal*
> *hope.*
>
> *And what is this impossible problem then?*
> *Only to give a few thousand people enough to eat,*
> *Decent houses and a fair income every week.*
> *What? For nothing? Yes! Scotland can well afford it.*
> *It cannot be done. The poor are always with us,*
> *The Bible says. Would other countries agree?*
> *Clearly we couldn't unless they did it too.*
> *All the old arguments against ending Slavery!*

All of this still rings true, even today as Scotland has its own

Parliament. This serious side was also accompanied by a biting wit. We must remember that MacDiarmid stood for parliament in a famous by-election in Kinross. He stood as a communist and a nationalist against Sir Alec Douglas-Home. I was at the Cross in Kinross when he berated the Tories for such lack of talent that they had had to exhume their candidate from the House of Lords.

But the frailties of man and woman have been reflected on by other poets. Today's scandal over MPs' expenses, and their duplicity or spin over events up to and including war, is alluded to in Norman MacCaig's gentle but thoughtful poem, 'A man in my position', whose first and final verses target all those whose only defence is that they were told that they were allowed to act dishonourably:

> *Hear my words carefully.*
> *Some are spoken*
> *not by me, but*
> *by a man in my position.*
>
> *Until he dies*
> *of my love for you*
> *hear my words carefully –*
> *for who is talking now?*

Art of Resistance pulls together the threads of a period of great creative endeavour in Scotland, which, due to the familiarity and friendship amongst the artistic fraternity, sometimes gives the nation the social flavour of a village. This is not a criticism but, in its own very Scottish way, its strength.

Henry McCubbin

Intruder

Susan Sontag, *Reborn: Early Diaries 1947-1964*, edited by David Rieff, Penguin, 318 pages, hardback ISBN 9780241144312, £16.99

I didn't know who Susan Sontag was before I read this book. Now, I feel I might know more than is desirable. The Preface by her only son, David Rieff, attracted me to Susan Sontag. She is presented as strong minded, opinionated, arrogant, independent, complicated and inspiring. David

Reiff was unsure whether to publish these intimate diaries, but felt his mother's character was so influential that either he 'would organise and present them or someone else would'. So he decided to publish them here in the first of three volumes, which catalogues her early experiences from the tender age of fifteen until thirty-one.

Reborn is filled with entries about the formation of the formidable individual who was Susan Sontag. Her thirst for knowledge, and her desire to escape from home to a life of intellectual stimulation, occupies much of the first two years. Once Sontag arrives at University, at the age of sixteen, her sexual desire for women occupies her thoughts and the page. She is childish about love and desire, which is to be expected of an inexperienced sixteen-year-old, but knowledgeable about books, music and who she is/wants to be. Her determination to be well read, and to understand what she is reading, adds to her precocity. However, this precociousness comes across as arrogance and intolerance towards others.

Susan Sontag does grow up during the sixteen years which *Reborn* covers. During the years of her marriage she writes more about philosophy, as well as the institution of marriage itself, and its limitations for her. She doesn't talk of her sexual desire throughout this period of her life, and seems dulled by the confines of her heterosexual union. Her diaries seem to characterize a freedom to explore herself – Susan Sontag uncovered – and become a place within which to note what constitutes her being.

Her openness and honesty is at times a little embarrassing, and as a reader I felt like an intruder, but a disinterested intruder at best. Had I studied some of her other works (such as *Regarding the Pain of Others*, which actually sounds interesting) before reading this collection of diaries I might have mustered more enthusiasm. I did, however, derive some enjoyment from Susan Sontag's inner monologue. She has lengthened my list of 'books to read'. For that I am appreciative.

Abi Rhodes

Communist Historians

Edited and introduced by David Parker, *Ideology, Absolutism and the English Revolution: Debates of the British Communist Historians 1940-1956*, Lawrence and Wishart, 288 pages, paperback ISBN 9781905007868, £18.99

Here is an outstanding collection of contributions by the most distinguished British Communist historians from 1940-1956. Christopher Hill, Eric Hobsbawm, Rodney Hilton, Maurice Dobb, Victor Kiernan, Roy Pascal and Brian Pearce figure among the great names, who will entice readers to pick up this remarkable record of a discussion on making sense of the English Revolution, which came to a head more than half a century ago. Early on the journey they will meet another famous name, that of R. Palme Dutt, who sought, on behalf of the Party, to lay down the parameters for a discussion which refused to be tamed by fiat. It must have felt like herding cats.

David Parker provides a lucid introduction to this book, which focuses our attention on the problem of Absolutism in defining the origins and the course of the English Revolution. David Parker has tracked down many of the original papers which emerged in this discussion over several years, and has published them with a comprehensive apparatus of notes which situates them in context.

Jim Smith

*　*　*

A Brown Study

Alexis Lykiard

In the prudent, doubtful playtime of a dourly downbeat Presbyter,
shifty bankers, shameless MPs, lived well on jam- and jelly-roll.
That grail Brown sought to inherit from Blair the pious predator
resembled a crock of old gilt, sold to a naked emperor;
dull years of waiting one's turn will tarnish the worthiest soul ...
When the Speaker scored an own goal, the rules spun right out of control:
lame excuses scuppered the strong – the Cup game went finally wrong.

June 2009

Alexis Lykiard's collection Unholy Empires *is available from Anarchios Press, PO Box 619, Exeter EX1 9JE, price £7.99.*